BEGINNERS GUIDE TO COMPANION PLANTING

GARDENING METHODS USING PLANT PARTNERS TO
GROW ORGANIC VEGETABLES

PETER SHEPPERD

CONTENTS

This checklist includes:

- 10 items you will need to kick off your green fingered adventure.
- The highest quality Gardening items.
- Where you can buy these items for the lowest price.

The last thing we want is for your gardening project start to be delayed because you weren't prepared.

To receive your essential tool checklist, visit the link:

www.petershepperd.com/gardening-checklist

INTRODUCTION

"A garden requires patient labour and attention. Plants do not grow merely to satisfy ambitions or to fulfil good intentions. They thrive because someone expended effort on them."

- Liberty Hyde Bailey

Most of us have grown up in a world that is dominated by intensive monoculture farming. Fields of maize, wheat, rice and barley not only dominate the landscapes of many states and countries, but also influence the way in which we have become accustomed to eating. Despite a dramatic increase in the range of vegetables and fruit on offer, we mainly survive on a small portion of those. It is true that we may have treats that sometimes fall outside of the traditional mainstay crops, but our diets are still dominated by those products that can be grown on a large-scale, commercial basis—wheat, rice and maize.

This eating to suit commercial production has widespread ramifications that nobody could have foreseen. As vast areas of land are dedicated to just one or two crops, soils become denuded of nutrients and the need for chemical fertilisers cannot be avoided. That, in turn, brings environmental repercussions, many of which are proving to be catastrophic. Closer to home, our more limited diets are depriving us of the vitamins and nutrients that we once consumed simply through eating so many different types of plant—a boon for the supplement manufacturers, but not so good for us.

This book is going to take a different approach to gardening. Instead of narrowing the selection of plants we eat, I aim to broaden that range dramatically and to do so using methods that were once common knowledge. Just like humans, plants thrive best in communities. The method of combining plants that bring benefits to one another is called companion planting. There is nothing new about it and, as you will see, in many parts of the world, it has been practiced for millennia.

Companion planting brings with it a multitude of different benefits, but they are all tied together by one underlying theme: the desire to harness nature, rather than trying to whip her into submission. Surely, the use of chemical fertilisers and pesticides has now gone on for long enough? We have seen disaster after disaster, watched the demise of bird and insect populations and stood by as vast swathes of our oceans are turned into dead zones. Now is the time to change that and to try to reverse some of the damage we have done to the planet.

This book does not offer a roadmap to doing this on a large scale. It does, however, offer you the possibility of doing what you can on a small scale, as an individual. You are not going to change the entire world by growing your own produce in harmony with nature, but you might change your own world. If enough people were to do the same, then the collective impact could be huge. The objective here is not just to increase the productivity of your vegetable garden, but to transform it into a mini ecosphere, where nature does much of the heavy lifting in terms of pest control and re-introduction of nutrients. We want it to be a place where life of many different types thrives, and not just a monocultural desert, devoid of all life, except for one or two crops.

I don't come at this subject waving a professorship in plant science or multiple degrees in horticulture. Instead, I want to share with you what more than a decade of organic gardening has taught me through trial and error. This is never going to be a subject that makes me into a multi-millionaire, but it is one about which I am passionate, and that combination of hands-on experience and deep passion must count for something.

I won't be delving too deeply into heavy science here. There are others far better qualified than I am to do that. Instead, I will take you on a journey that I have been on for many years. It is speckled with pitfalls and disasters that sometimes occur when you work with nature, but when you harvest your first warm tomato or pull that first succulent, homegrown carrot from the earth, those problems are quickly forgotten. I hope this book will teach you all about the subject of companion planting and its many benefits and at the same time, that it will help you to avoid some of the errors that I made on my own journey. Above all, I hope that it will inspire you and that you will come away as passionate about organic gardening as I am. If that happens, you will never look at the food on your plate in quite the same way again.

Companion planting is a broad subject and, as is often the case when delving into a new field, it can seem a little overwhelming. Right from the start, I want to point out that this can be something you introduce to your gardening gradually. You can try a combination or two here and there and then, if you are happy with the results, build on it the following year. Little by little, both your knowledge and your skills will start to increase. You will also experience a dramatic growth in self-confidence when it comes to gardening. Feel free to use this information in bite-sized chunks, rather than treating it as one gastronomic meal.

1

WHO'S THE RIGHT COMPANION FOR YOUR PLANT?

Companion planting can be carried out for one of several reasons. Some plants act as a deterrent for pests, while others might be grown to attract beneficial insects. Some plants provide food or accommodation to pollinators, while others bind nutrients into the soil and therefore increase yields. We might also use companion planting simply because it makes more sense to plant one plant alongside another, purely to save space. Like so much to do with nature, the subject is interlinked and woven together in its own intricate ecosystem, and it is the gardener's job to find the best way to harness those interplant connections.

We hear a great deal about monoculture, because it has become so prevalent in modern agriculture. The opposite of monoculture is polyculture and we hear far less about that, even though it was being practiced long before anyone really thought about simply growing one crop at a time to maximise profits. If we do stumble across the term, it is often in association with bearded hippy types who we might think have rolled one too many joints.

Image 1. Polyculture garden bed

They appear to have wandered out of conventional borders and strayed into the territory that most of society deems weird. In fact, individuals of such slightly weird fringe elements have often proven to be the best pioneers when it comes to rediscovering the lost art of organic cultivation. I am not suggesting you have to go all "Kumbaya" and grow dreadlocks, but you might want to spare some respect for people that bucked social norms in order to put the environment first.

Polyculture predates the hippy era of the late sixties and seventies by some centuries. It first began in Belize, Costa Rica, Nicaragua, El Salvador, Guatemala and Honduras in an area that historians refer to as Mesoamerica. In terms of plant cultivation, this is where it all began. Here people first started to abandon the hunter-gatherer lifestyle in around 7000 BC, as they started to get to grips with cultivating plants such as maize, tomatoes, avocados, squash and chilis. Modern colonisation saw those crops being exported all over the world and some experts suggest that up to three-fifths of the plants that make up the modern diet can find their origins in Mesoamerica. Those early agriculturists did not try to focus just on one crop, but instead grew a wide variety of plants in conjunction with one another.

They were not influenced by profit-making, but simply wanted to have enough food to survive and it made sense to hedge their bets by growing a range of produce. More recently, in China, a mere thousand or so years ago, farmers started to grow rice in conjunction with a fern called the mosquito fern. This plant served two purposes: on the one hand, the ferns blocked out light to plants competing with the rice, and on the other, they fixed nitrogen, thus keeping the soil high in

Figure 2. Rice field surrounded by the Mosquito Fern

nutrients. Very often you will see that companion planting offers more than one benefit to a specific crop.

Those early Chinese agriculturists would have had no way of knowing that the nodules on the roots of the mosquito fern were useful in sequestering nitrogen. All they would have known then was that when they grew one plant with the other, they obtained a better yield.

By the time European colonists first hit the shores of modern-day America, the native Americans were already using a system known as The Three Sisters. Into one hole they would drop a corn seed, a squash seed and a bean seed.

The beans would use the corn as a climbing support, while at the same time binding nitrogen into the soil. The squash would spread and act as a living mulch as its leaves denied sunlight to the weeds that would have thrived without their presence. The three-plant combination yielded three crops in one space, which all bene-fitted one another in a classic example of companion planting. It probably wasn't very neat, but that was not their objective. They were purely focused on a practical arrangement that saved them time and offered a better yield. I am of the belief that our fascination with neat-ness may have had a detri-mental effect on basic gardening when it comes to food production.

The English cottage garden system has become some-thing of a contemporary gardening style in the last few decades. Today it is often used simply to combine orna-mental plants in an eye-pleasing manner, but that was

Figure 3. Bean flower climbing over a corn plant

not always the case. One theory about its origins is that following the Black Death in 1340, so much land became vacant that labourers were able to start inten-sively cultivating small pieces of ground. With the shortage of available labour following the mass deaths of the plague, large landowners would try to entice workers to their estates by offering cottages with small pieces of ground attached. While the men were working the fields, these gardens were often tended by their wives, who planted an eclectic mixture of fruit, vegetables and ornamental plants. They were not restrained by any rules, because they simply did not know any rules. Instead, they went with what worked. In modern terms, this is just another variant of a very ancient method of growing plants, but it shows that companion planting has some pedigree to it and is not just the latest in a long series of gardening trends.

For the home gardener, getting to grips with which plants best complement one another can be a little complicated and this book will try to unravel some of that mystery for you. Here, we will focus mainly on edible plants, but later in the series, we will be looking more deeply into town gardens, and there we will also consider plant combinations from a more ornamental point of view. It is perfectly feasible to grow both food crops and ornamental crops together and I believe that that is one trend we will see far more of over the coming years. People are becoming more aware of what they eat and that is seeing a tidal wave of back-yard farmers who want at least to augment their supermarket-supplied food with vegetables they have grown themselves. In short, they want greater control of what goes into their crops and therefore onto their plates. It is also not simply a health concern. Sure, most people don't want to eat plants that have been treated with chemicals, but food from the home garden often just tastes better. It hasn't travelled thousands of miles or sat on a supermarket shelf for several days or weeks.

Another factor is that we are slowly starting to let go of the idea that food plants are grown here and ornamental plants are grown there. Many vegetables and herbs are handsome plants in their own right. Why shouldn't they be included in the ornamental garden and then harvested when ready to eat? Likewise, flowers attract pollinators and deter pests and can serve a purpose in the vegetable garden. Gradually we are starting to see a blurring of the boundaries between the ornamental and the edible areas that we cultivate. I must confess that in my own garden the two areas are still quite distinct, but when I look back at some of my early planting plans, I am often quite surprised at how many plants have crept from one region to another. There are different methods employed by the serious companion planter and some of them vary quite considerably.

Nasturtiums, for example, are frequently grown in the vicinity of brassica crops such as cabbages, cauliflower or broccoli. The brassica family are prone to attack by the caterpillar of the cabbage white butterfly. The idea here is that the butterflies will preferentially lay their eggs on the leaves of the nasturtiums and that this will reduce the threat they pose to the brassica crop in question.

When used in this way, the nasturtium becomes a sacrificial plant. Strangely enough, people are also rediscovering the nasturtium leaf as a spicy additive to salads and it too, is becoming more popular as an edible plant. Butter some bread and slap a few nasturtium leaves on it and you have a rather nice sandwich that was once widely enjoyed, but somehow got lost in our constantly evolving culinary

Figure 4. A flowering perennial herbaceous Nasturtium

Figure 5. Sacrificial Nasturtium and Marigolds used as trap crops for cabbage

history.

You will sometimes see marigolds growing amongst beds or along borders, particularly where the crop is tomatoes. The strong-smelling flowers attract beneficial insects such as ladybirds and hoverflies. At varying stages in their life cycles, these insects feed happily on greenfly and aphids which are a threat to the crop. By attracting predators, they reduce the threat from the pests and at the same time, the gardener hopes to attract bees, which will aid with pollination. In this case, the companion plant is not sacrificial, but beneficial, and can serve more than one purpose. It attracts predatory insects, as well as bees and other pollinators, whilst being pleasing to the eye.

As anyone who grows carrots will know, carrot fly can be a major nuisance. These low-flying flies lay their eggs at the base of the plant and their grubs then munch their way into the carrot itself. Often, the gardener won't even be aware that the plant he is so carefully nurturing is acting as a diner for grubs, until harvest time. Plants such as garlic and onions act as a deterrent. We are unsure if the flies dislike the smell of these plants or if their strong odour simply prevents the fly from being able to locate the carrot itself. Who cares? All we want is strong, healthy carrots.

Not all companion planting relates to pests and beneficial insects. Some plants can be grown together purely for physical factors.

Corn and sunflowers both provide wonderful living trellises for climbing plants such as beans, peas and even cucumbers. Tomatoes not only produce delicious fruit; they can also provide dappled shade that will be a benefit to plants such as spinach and chard.

Figure 6. Sunflower trellis

Later in this book, we will look in greater depth into the different types of companion plants and the reasons for using them. There will be some charts for you to use, which will provide you with a guide as to which plants are known to grow well alongside which other plants. Please don't feel bound to follow any of these systems. They will help, but each garden is different in terms of pests that pose a problem, soil nutrients and crops that are being cultivated. This is not a process of rigid rules; instead, you are free to experiment and see what works best for you. Here, it is worth mentioning that there is a wealth of information to be gained from other gardeners in your area, who will have the most in-depth knowledge of local conditions. It is difficult to overstress how valuable this information can be.

There was a time when, if you were intent on going down the organic route, you would be somewhat frowned upon by old boys who had grown up using chemical fertilizers and blasting the insect population into submission through the lavish use of pesticides. Just the mention of bucking this trend would have had them shaking their heads and tut-tutting in contempt. On some allotments, some of them would be openly hostile to your subversive techniques. You always left these encounters confident in the knowledge that they would be laughing at you behind your back.

Today, I am pleased to say that all of that has definitely changed. Most of those old hands have died out (probably through chemical poisoning) and most small-scale vegetable growers are organic to one degree or another. In fact, there is sometimes a certain amount of one-upmanship which might see one gardener trying to outdo another in a bizarre effort to be greener than anyone else. I suggest you find those whose environmental beliefs align most closely with yours and then mercilessly milk them for information. You will be surprised at just how sharing the gardening community can be. It is quite refreshing in the cut-throat and self-centered society we live in. If there is a local gardening club or community garden, then you would be well-advised to participate. It may take up some of your time, but the information exchange, seed swaps and sharing of produce will more than make up for it. You may even be surprised to discover that some of those crinkly garden types are actually quite nice people as well. A quick word of warning here – try not to get drawn into purist debates about whose green credentials are stronger than whose. It's a slippery slope and no matter how green you become, there will always be someone who goes one step greener. If you have ever listened to a vegan arguing with a vegetarian, you will know what I mean. I feel that we serve ourselves and the gardening community far better by helping one another, rather than by condemning practices that don't live up to our standards. Lead and learn by example, rather than espousing dogma.

With companion planting, you will need to train yourself to look more at the big picture than at the individual crop. What you are endeavouring to create is a balanced ecosystem in which there are fewer pests, greater nutrient retention and more vitamins and minerals in the harvest itself. At first, this may seem to be logical, but it flies in the face of commercial gardening, which supplies most of the food you have been eating up until now. In the commercial world, the objective is not to have fewer pests: the objective is to have none, and therefore to use whatever method necessary to wipe them off the face of the Earth. Never mind if their extinction creates a gap in the environment for another pest to fill. There will be, the theory goes, another chemical with which to destroy that pest too.

Little attention is paid to interconnectivity in the commercial world. The fact that we are suffering huge drops in the number of wild birds, due to a reduction in insects, doesn't really seem to keep these people awake at night. Nor do they seem particularly concerned that when we poison pests, we almost always end up poisoning beneficial insects at the same time. They are more concerned about turning a buck and that attitude is enhanced now that so many big corporate producers are no longer privately owned. They answer to distant shareholders, rather than an ailing environment. Somehow, the fact that we may be a part of this complex interconnected ecosystem seems to have slipped their minds. You and I can do little to change that. All we can do is carve out a more sustainable path for ourselves and our families.

The ethos behind companion planting, and indeed the organic movement as a whole, is not one that attempts to totally destroy any part of the environment. Instead, the belief is that the environment is a cohesive whole and that the best that we can hope for is to be able to manage it in a way that brings wins for both ourselves and the ecosystem. This means that we need to accept that there will be a certain amount of loss due to the presence of pests. Many writers tend to gloss over this little glitch and give the impression that organic farming or vegetable growing is a cure-all method that will enable the grower to produce wonderfully healthy crops, whilst at the same time, not having to pay any price to the environment.

Organic growing is a constant juggling act in which you try to maintain a perfectly healthy environment on the one hand, and produce maximum yields on the other. Companion planting is one very powerful tool towards doing this. It is not, however, by any means perfect. Commercial organic farmers have had to come to accept that, on average, their yields will be 30% lower than those of commercial farmers armed with a battery of pesticides and chemical fertilizers. What we are starting to see is an increase in those yields, which is facilitated by a number of factors. Growers are becoming more aware of varieties and cultivars that are hardier to their individual circumstances, soil management skills without chemical fertilizers are becoming better and the overall health of many soils in these environments is improving. All of this is acting as a strong beacon of hope for the organic farming and gardening movement. It is difficult to measure how much benefit the organic gardener gains as the ecosystem in his small farm or garden reaches a balance. In my own case, I am seeing steadily rising yields, which I attribute to the balance being far better than it was when I first started moving my garden towards becoming chemical-free.

Figure 7. The sweet nectar of Borage is great to attract useful pollinators

I believe that it will be many years before we will see the organic producer showing yields as high as those of farmers using chemicals and pesticides and who focus on just one or two crops. At the same time, I firmly believe that even with reduced yields, the benefits in terms of both the ecosystem and the quality of the produce generated outweighs the excess produced by the commercial farmer.

Realistically, I think you need to prepare yourself for the fact that if you are going to improve the health of the small ecosystem that you control, then it is going to impact, to a certain extent, what you will be able to produce. Personally, my experience has shown me that the improved environment within my own garden, and the quality of the vegetables that I am producing, more than outweigh the losses that I have sustained had I been using chemicals for either fertilizing or pest control. My own experience seems to be backed up by the ever-increasing number of organic gardeners that we see today. It is a movement that is gathering steam, slowly but surely, aided by a more informed consumer and a desire to leave this planet in a better state than it was in when we inherited it.

Finally, I would like to point out that each season, the natural equilibrium within my garden seems to be gradually reaching a balance. Each year, the number of beneficial insects seems to increase, whilst the number of pests seems to decrease. Many organic gardeners find they have similar results when they first convert to gardening without chemicals. At first, the yield drops, due largely to pests. Later, as the ecosystem becomes established and a natural balance is achieved, the yields creep back up again. This time, however, the yield is healthier produce, free of chemical residue of any kind. Years of enhancing my soil using compost and manure mean that it now seems to be reaching peak performance. That, combined with the fact that I am gradually becoming better and better at my choice of companion plants, means that my yields are going up year on year. This is something of which, I have to admit, I am actually quite proud.

2

THE FUNDAMENTAL PILLARS OF COMPANION PLANTING

Although man has been practicing companion planting for millennia, it should be noted that it still remains a relatively unstudied field in terms of modern science. Much of what you will be doing in your own garden will, in fact, be pioneering work, even though you may not wish to be so adventurous. In the appendix section of this book will present some tables offering a wide variety of companion planting options, but, as with all gardening, some of what you will be doing will be a matter of trial and error—a sort of wild experiment that is all part of the gardening adventure.

As a rule of thumb, companion planting should benefit all plants that are grown together in combination with one another. In the last chapter, we looked at the example of the Three Sisters, which was so heavily favoured by native Americans.

Figure 8. Corn vegetable garden

In that example, all three plants, the corn, the beans and the squash, shared advantages from one another that contributed to the wellbeing of the plants and the overall yield. More realistically, there are often instances where we combine plants in which the combination is not beneficial to all of them. Using nasturtiums to draw caterpillars away from brassicas, for example, offers little in the way of benefit for the nasturtium. One could argue, of course, that were the nasturtium not so useful, it would not have been included in the vegetable garden in the first place, so perhaps it does benefit it, in a more roundabout way.

There are also combinations of plants that simply work against one another. For example, it would be a bad idea to plant a water-loving plant alongside one that prefers drier conditions. This might seem obvious, but with all the different factors to take into account when choosing plant partnerships, it is easy to overlook something so crucial. As we work through this book, we will be taking a more in-depth look at plants that should not be planted together and some of the reasons why. For the time being, we will focus on those plant relationships that do work. There are four main factors that are generally taken into account when deciding on which companion plants to combine. These are often referred to as the "pillars of companion planting".

The first method, and one which is fairly reliable, is to stick with plants of the same botanical family. Although not always the case, it is very often true that plants from the same family share similar growing require-ments. Alliums, such as onions and garlic, share many of the same growing requirements and it makes sense to intercrop them. If you also plant them in the vicinity of your carrots, you will reap yet another benefit: they are good crops for shielding carrots from carrot fly. Plants that share common cultivation requirements can make a gardener's life much easier if they are all grown near to one another. You can water and feed them both at the same rate and time.

Figure 9. Alliums shield other crops from carrot fly

While combining plants through the use of their botanical families is one reliable method of deciding on companion plants, there are others that you should consider. If you combine plants on the basis of their feeding requirements, you are often able to make the best possible use of your soil. In some instances, or at least in some beds, the soil may be richer than it is in others. There could be a number of reasons for this: you may not have been practicing ideal crop rotation methods and the soils could have been depleted, or you may simply have fed one bed with more compost or manure than another. Cucumbers, tomatoes and squash are all heavy feeders and they would benefit from a richer soil, whilst crops like beets, carrots, turnips and onions thrive perfectly happily in relatively poor soils. Once you know and understand the soil conditions that you have, you are better able to consider the vegetables that you should plant. You will also need to learn which plants are heavy feeders and which ones require lower amounts of nutrients to perform well. The combination of those two pieces of information will better enable you to choose which plants to intercrop with one another.

The third method is to combine plants where the physical attributes of one may offer benefits to another. We have already looked at using corn as a climbing support for beans, but it is also common to plant lettuce in the shade of sunflowers or tomatoes, thus keeping them cooler than if they were planted in full sun.

Lettuce are cool-weather plants that perform at their best during the shoulder seasons of spring and autumn. If they are lightly shaded, then you can extend that season. Plants like squash that run along the ground may take up a lot of space, but the foliage can act as a mulch. If cleverly combined with crops that ripen early, the combination crop may very well be reaped before the heavy foliage becomes dense enough to swamp it. The final method that is most commonly used when drawing up plant combinations is to defend against pests. We have seen how onions and garlic can deter carrot fly, but there are many other combinations that provide a similar benefit. For example, bush beans planted near to potatoes have been shown to considerably reduce infestations of the dreaded Colorado beetle that so many potato growers have come to

Figure 10. Pumping foliage is great as mulch

hate. Personally, this is the main way in which I use companion planting in my own garden.

As you can now see, these four methods offer a wide variety of different combinations for companion planting. If you then mix and match them to your own specific gardening needs, the plant combinations you can come up with grows significantly. That is why I am hesitant to prescribe combinations that might lead a newer gardener to believe that there are hard and fast rules that must be adhered to. By all means, refer to the tables in the appendix in this regard, but never lose sight of the fact that your own conditions, soil type and vegetable choices must influence your decisions. This will mean that how you choose to combine plants becomes fairly unique to you and your garden. Don't worry if I am being too general at the moment. I want you to be clear about why you are doing this and then in the next chapter we will delve more deeply into what to grow with what and which combinations to avoid.

In addition to the four pillars of companion planting listed above, you will also want to start including other plants for slightly different reasons. Many annuals and perennials that have a long flowering period are great for attracting beneficial insects to your garden. Having these plants dotted about the garden can bring huge benefits, in that they attract pollinators or predatory insects that feed on common garden pests. Though these plants bring little in the way of crop return, they still increase yields in ways that are probably impossible to measure. When a growing system is established on a foundation of best organic principles, diversity becomes far more important than it would be in a situation where pesticides can be freely used.

The important thing is that you are clear in your own mind as to why you are combining specific plants. While, in an ideal world, a gardener would always combine two or more plants that benefit one another, it is often the case that when you plant two plants together, the benefit goes mainly to one plant and not the other. Poached egg plants are often intercropped with vegetables.

Figure 11. Companion planting of home grown organic Potatoes and Poached Egg plants

They attract pests away from the vegetable crop, but reap no reward in return. They are known as a sacrificial partner. The fact that one plant is benefiting and another isn't is no reason to invalidate that pairing or assume it is not a good combination.

Wine producers have been doing something similar for years. Very often you will see rose bushes growing at the end of long rows of vines. This is not for the aesthetic benefits that the roses offer. The rose attracts aphids more quickly than the vines do and they are also quicker to become infected with fungal disease. By keeping an eye on the health of the rose, the wine producer gets an early warning alert as to any problems that may soon threaten their vines.

Overall, most of the combinations that a gardener will choose will almost inevitably result in a greater diversity of plants in the garden. The one big advantage of this is that it eliminates, or at least vastly reduces, the possibility of total crop loss. While you are almost bound to have your failings here and there, what turns out as a loss on one hand may well turn out as a gain on another. There seems to be a sort of universal commonality when it comes to gardening in this way. In any given year, you may get virtually no corn, whilst at the same time having a bumper harvest of another crop such as tomatoes. That, I'm afraid, is part and parcel of the gardening game. It does mean that, come the harvest season, you often have a glut of one type of vegetable or another. In the last book on 'advanced raised bed gardening', I took a long look at some of the various techniques for storing food when you have such a glut. If you are hoping to get anywhere near the point of self-sufficiency, understanding the different methods of preserving excess harvest is crucial. Having some sort of an association with other gardeners is also useful here. If you have an excess of one product and another gardener has an excess of another, it leads to an obvious opportunity to plant-swap.

Where the monoculture system has become widely practiced, it also exposes us to huge risks of overall crop failure, as was demonstrated so clearly during the Irish Potato Famine. By incorporating many different plants into your garden and using a wide variety of companion planting methods, you are at far less risk of total crop failure. In essence, what you are doing is spreading your bets.

Biodiversity and companion planting are two sides of the same coin. Having a wider range of plants available means that the gardener is far less exposed to risks from disease, pests and weather conditions than is the monoculture farmer. In monoculture, all the farmer's eggs are in one basket. He must defend that basket with the widescale use of pesticides and fortify it with chemical fertilisers. Currently, that system is working for large-scale commercial farmers who are producing huge yields. Such yields offer economies of scale. One combine harvester, for example, can harvest huge swathes of grain crops. If the field were divided to support many different types of plant, then that machine would cease to be so beneficial. Those yields are not coming without a price, however. Our soils are becoming degraded, insect and bird populations are being decimated and our diets are now dominated by a relatively small group of plants. As a small-scale gardener with a wide variety of plants, that situation is reversed. What you are doing makes sense not just for you as the gardener, but for the environment as a whole. You are aiding biodiversity and improving the environment, rather than simply looting it. This ability to grow your own produce and still give something back to Mother Nature is both rewarding to the gardener and important to the natural world.

Botanists tell us that there are more than 400,000 different species of plant on the planet and they suspect that around 300,000 of those are edible, and yet we eat from a bland list of just two hundred different types of plant. It gets even worse than that when you realise that just three grain crops, wheat, rice and maize, make up more than fifty per cent of the plant calories that we consume. By broadening the range of plants that we eat, we not only add diversity to our diets, but also to the ecosystems in the garden. Sure, we need to stick to what we know to be sure of a yield in some circumstances, but I also dedicate a section of my garden to what I call "experiments". These experiments might be crazy seeds that I found in a catalogue or plantlets I was given by one of my equally adventurous gardening friends. Often the experiments end in failure, but every now and then, I stumble on a gem of a plant that will go on to make it onto my regular planting list, and my plate, year after year. Be bold and think outside of the box. You might just surprise yourself with what you can achieve.

In the next chapter, we will get down to the nuts and bolts of which plants to combine.

3

EXAMPLES OF GOOD AND BAD NEIGHBOURS

B y now you should have a pretty good idea of why the organic gardener makes such widespread use of companion planting. In this chapter, we will delve more deeply into plant combinations and some of the many options that have already been tried and tested. That said, you should definitely not believe that these are the only combinations available or that they will be perfect in your own garden. Instead, treat them as a general guideline and then be prepared to make changes to suit yourself where necessary.

Some gardeners become quite upset when they discover how few hard and fast rules there are when it comes to the cultivation of plants. Personally, it is that ability to stamp my personal mark on a garden that makes the subject so interesting to me. Each garden is a delicate arrangement of soils, microclimate, and plant combinations and as such, sticking to a hard set of rules can actually be a mistake. You need to think of the garden in the same way you would a blank canvas if you were painting a picture.

Figure 12. Every garden tells a wonderful story

There will always be basic rules in terms of the materials, techniques and use of perspective, but from then on it is your individual creativity and ingenuity that will determine whether you end up with a beautiful picture or not. Gardening is part science and part art and quite how you combine those two aspects will dictate your progress. No matter how much experience you have, and regardless of how much you study the subject, gardening will always contain an element of the unknown. At the end of the day, it is always worth reminding yourself that Mother Nature has the controlling hand. No two seasons are the same, each variety of plant performs differently and our soils are seldom consistent. In short, gardening can be a bit of a rollercoaster ride, but that rollercoaster ride provides the adventure that makes the subject so addictive.

Now let's move ahead and take a more in-depth look at some of the plants most commonly used in companion planting combinations. Though these may have worked well for other gardeners, consider them and experiment with them but don't feel bound by them.

Companion planting takes a slight change in mindset to the traditional vegetable garden planting that you have probably always been accustomed to. What you're trying to do now is create communities of plants that benefit one another and avoid those traditional rows and blocks of plants. Think of it this way: if you are a flying pest and you see a long and inviting row of your favourite vegetables laid out in front of you, how much more tempting is that going to be than if you have to manoeuvre around plants that aren't to your taste or that may harbour other insects who might fancy eating you? Likewise, a caterpillar will find it far easier to chew his way along a row of lettuce or cabbages than it will if the plants are interspersed with other vegetables that he finds inedible.

Flowering plants inserted randomly into these patches of vegetables break up the consistency and are thought to confuse many insects. Herbs such as mint, parsley, tansy and catnip are all deterrents for pests and can be easily inserted into beds in random places. Some of these herbs, such as mint, might become a little bit of invasive when planted into ideal growing conditions like your beds. What I tend to do, is grow them in pots which I can then place in the garden where needed and move them when their anti-pest properties are required elsewhere. In this way, I have a mobile pest deterrent that just happens to be edible at the same time.

Most of the leguminous plants, such as beans and peas, have nodules on the roots which have been proven to lock nitrogen into the soil. This is quite a neat little trick, and one that wise gardeners have been quick to utilize. In a symbiotic relationship between plants and soil-based bacteria, the bacteria trap nitrogen gas, which they feed to the plant via their nodules. In return, they gather carbohydrates from the plant as payback. Excess nitrogen becomes fixed in the soil during the exchange.

As nitrogen is one of the most important nutrients for vegetables, this is important knowledge to have, because it enables the gardener to ensure that his or her soils are rich in this valuable nutrient. Remember that companion planting is just a tool to aid the achievement of better gardening success, and that it will never eliminate the need for very healthy soil. Understanding soil is important for the gardener because if he or she understands any deficiencies, it will help him or her in his or her choice of companion plants. We will be looking more at soil types and characteristics in the other books in this series.

Flowering friends

There are many flowering plants that can be used as companion plants in the vegetable garden, despite the fact that they often don't actually offer any harvestable return themselves. The flowering plants in the list below, you are going to see being used again and again. We will take a deeper look at them as well as some easy ways in which to propagate them so that you can always produce your own supply of these most common allies.

The common **poached eggplant** is a great flower to grow amongst your vegetables, as it attracts hoverflies, which are ferocious insect predators. These plants are annuals, which, in addition to attracting beneficial insects, also provide a delightful flash of colour in places where it might not be expected, and which always make people smile. They self-sow freely but are not pushy, so won't become invasive. The seedlings will come through in autumn and can be left in place as a cover crop and then simply dug into the soil come the spring. If you want to keep some of the seedlings, rather than resowing in the spring, then protect them over winter and they will quickly flower when the weather warms up. You can do this by covering them with a fleece or some straw during the winter months.

Propagating: These plants are very easy to grow and if you are looking to get young children interested in gardening, then this is an ideal plant to generate enthusiasm. They will tolerate most soils but it is best to dig the ground over, mix in some well-rotted

Figure 13. A colourful blooming Poached Eggplant

compost and rake to a fine tilth before sowing directly in situ.

Plant the seeds about four inches apart and a half an inch deep in the spring. Water in using a fine rose on a watering can or a garden wand. Once the seedlings start to show signs of becoming sturdy, then simply thin them to about four inches apart and there you have it. You can transplant the thinned seedlings elsewhere or into any gaps. The speed of growth and minimal effort really helps to get kids interested in the gardening process. Once you point to the insects they attract, they start to understand the role they play as companion plants and it further stimulates their interest into the garden ecosystem as a whole.

Borage is another flowering plant that you will frequently see used as a companion plant. It helps to bind minerals into the soil, but is also excellent for attracting bees and therefore makes a perfect companion plant for tomatoes, where pollination is so important. Borage used to be used in ancient medicine in poultices for the healing of broken bones and you will still hear older gardeners refer to it as 'heal bone.'

Figure 14. Borage seed oil used for many cosmetic remedies

In addition to being a great companion plant, the leaves can be used as a supplementary food, either as a fertilizer tea or by simply adding them to your compost heap. These plants can be very vigorous, so choose the position in which you plant them carefully.

Propagation: Borage is best grown from seed in situ, just after the last frosts have passed. It doesn't transplant well, so it is best to sow it directly to its final growing position. Take into consideration that these plants are free-seeding once established and can spread their seeds to around four feet.

Prepare the soil by digging it over, mixing in a layer of compost and then raking to a fine tilth. Sow seeds about twelve inches apart and just lightly cover them with a layer of soil that shouldn't be more than a quarter of an inch deep. Water them in with a fine spray and keep the soil moist, but not soggy.

The **marigold** has long been rated as a flowering plant that offers powerful pest-repellent properties. Any gardener who has had anything to do with these brightly coloured little flowers will be aware of the strong odour that they emit. Generally, you will come across two fairly distinct varieties, the African and the French. Both originate from Mexico, which is just another of those horticultural mysteries designed to complicate your life. I always opt for the French varieties, which are more compact but also flower for longer. Feel free to choose whichever variety you prefer, as they all have that distinct smell that insects dislike. In fact, these plants are so easy to grow that they are often the first plants that children are taught to sow.

Figure 15. Marigold flowers

They will flower right through from spring until the first frosts, so they offer long-term protection. Whilst beneficial in most garden situations, they don't appear to get on well with peas or beans.

Propagation: African marigolds are tall and French marigolds are much shorter. They are both easy to grow and the seeds are cheap, so you might want to consider growing both so that you can take advantage of their benefits as a pest deterrent at differing heights.

Sow seeds in cells of potting soil four to six weeks before the spring, so that they are ready to plant out as soon as the last frosts have passed. They don't need to be sown deeply but should just be lightly covered with soil and watered in. Sow two to three of the black and white coloured seeds per cell. Place the tray on a sunny windowsill and they should emerge within three to four days. Thin them to one seed per cell when the first true leaves appear and as soon as they are a little sturdier, they can be potted on into small individual containers, to be planted out when the weather warms. At the end of the season, gather some of the dead flower heads and allow them to dry before collecting your own seed for the season to come.

Nasturtiums are one of the better-known flowering plants that provide good insect protection. Although native to Colombia, Bolivia and Peru, the nasturtium is frequently called Indian cress (yet another of those little horticultural anomalies that we gardeners have to deal with). They have been grown in Europe since the 16th century, when Spanish conquistadors brought them back from the Americas.

Their peppery-tasting leaves make a spicy additive for salads and, when pickled in vinegar, the seeds become very much like capers. They are a vigorously trailing plant, which can be quite handy if you are trying to hide some garden eyesore or other.

They deter whitefly, cucumber beetle, squash beetle and Colorado beetle and they make excellent companion plants when grown amongst brassicas, cucumbers, radishes or tomatoes. One thing you need to be aware of if you're growing these plants for their flowers is that they thrive in poor soil. If you feed them or grow them in too rich a soil, they will produce abundant foliage, but reduce the number of flowers that they put out.

Figure 16. Summer Nasturtium soup delicious hot or cold

I find this plant particularly useful when grown amongst broad beans. Broad beans are one of the first vegetables to ripen in the garden and are therefore a valuable crop for breaking the winter hunger period. Unfortunately, there are a few plants that I know of that are more attractive to blackfly. Nasturtiums provide a useful companion plant to help to reduce this problem. To be fair, I have never totally eradicated blackfly by using nasturtiums as a companion plant. What they do is minimise the infestations to a point where I am able to control them quite easily with the use of vegetable soap or another organic pesticide. Quite frequently, this sort of thing occurs with companion planting. You don't always achieve total protection, but what you do gain is an element of protection that makes eliminating the pest a much more manageable task.

Propagation: Another plant that is really easy to propagate, nasturtiums can be grown from cuttings, but they are so simple to grow from seed that taking cuttings really is not necessary. There are over fifty varieties of nasturtium with a wide selection of both colour and flower shape. They range in colour from almost black, right through to pale yellow. Although the choice is wide, nasturtiums can basically be broken down into three types: low trailing or climbing. Once you have decided what form you want your plants to take, it is just a matter of taste as to which variety you go for.

Plant your seeds into small pots or cell trays about four weeks before the last frosts are expected. These plants place few demands on the soil and will thrive in soil that is quite poor. You can even use old potting soil from the previous season, though this is regarded as a big no-no in the gardening world, so don't tell anyone that you got that idea from me. The seeds are large and easy to manipulate so sow just one per cell and to a depth of about three times the diameter of the seed. Water them in and place them on a south-facing windowsill and they should germinate within a week. By ten days, they will be exhibiting their first true leaves.

These plants are not frost-tolerant, so you are going to need to keep them in a protected environment until you are sure there is little risk of frost. If they are starting to get too big for their cells or pots you may need to pot them into a bigger container during this time. As soon as the weather warms, they can be planted directly into your beds. They self-seed very easily, so you may have self-sown plants the next season, or you can gather your own seed as soon as it is dry. You need to be aware, though, that not all seed will give the exact same result the following season, if they are F1 hybrids. Nasturtiums are another flowering plant that can really encourage kids to get into gardening, so they are a useful plant for parents who are keen to share their passion for this activity.

Calendula is another all-round good guy to incorporate into your vegetable garden. You'll often hear them referred to as pot marigolds. Although they are not marigolds at all, they are members of the same daisy family. Like many of the flowering companion plants that we will use regularly in our vegetable gardens, they are easy to grow and, left to their own devices, will self-seed quite freely. If you prefer to have your seedlings appear in a more organized fashion, then harvest some of the seed heads, dry them out and simply plant them where you want them the following spring.

Figure 17. Organic Calendula soap

They serve a dual purpose in the garden in that they discourage predatory insects, but remain a favourite with pollinators. There are dozens of different varieties to choose from, but don't let this confuse you. Simply opt for the ones that you find most pleasing. If you deadhead them regularly throughout the growing season, they will reward you with more flowers after each cutting. As an added bonus, these flowers have numerous culinary uses and can be used to brighten summer salads. A few of them tied together with simple gardener's twine makes a wonderful bouquet, which can become very useful for calming an angry wife when she discovers you've walked garden soil across her new carpet. Plant flowers near to salad crops, cucumbers, tomatoes, peas and carrots.

Propagation: Calendula is easy to grow by sowing seeds directly into the beds in the vicinity of the plants you want them to be combined with. They do best if they get off to a cool start, so plant them in spring, but about one or two weeks before the last frosts. Germination can be inhibited by light, so plant them half an inch deep in a well-prepared soil and keep them between twelve and fifteen inches apart. By early summer, they will have started to produce what is the start of an abundance of flowers. Deadheading will encourage them to set more blooms and they can keep on flowering until after the first frosts at the end of autumn.

You will need to keep the soil moist, so expect to water once or twice a week during the drier months. To produce such an abundance of flowers requires plenty of nutrients, so apply a liquid feed once a month. These plants are great self-seeders and you will have plenty of seedlings the following season, though these might not necessarily grow where you need them to. If you cut off one or two of the flower heads just before they dry, you can lay them on a sheet of paper in a cool dry place.

When they finish drying out, just shake out the curled, light brown seeds and store them in an envelope or paper bag. Sow them where you want to the following season.

Lavender is a shrub that I'm sure every gardener is familiar with. Hardy, easy to grow and pleasing to the eye, this is the plant that many people don't think of in terms of companion planting. There are many different varieties and some get much bigger than others. Most don't lend themselves to being squeezed into beds amongst vegetables, but they can be dotted here and there in the vegetable garden, or used to create attractive hedging on the borders.

Whole books have been written on the subject of lavender and its many uses to man, so I won't delve too deeply into that. As far as companion planting is concerned, there are few flowering plants that bees, butterflies and other pollinators find more seductive. At the same time, whitefly and aphids cannot stand them. They get on well with most vegetable plants and are particularly useful when planted near to tomatoes.

Propagation: You can grow lavender from seed but it is a slow and sometimes unreliable process. You are far better off taking cuttings and here you have two options. Softwood cuttings are taken using new growth in the spring and hardwood cuttings can be taken during the summer. Although softwood cuttings are quicker to take, they tend not to be as reliable and so I prefer to take hardwood cuttings, though the methodology is pretty much the same. Softwood cuttings are taken using soft new growth whilst hardwood cuttings use older, more mature plant material that has turned woody.

Look for healthy growing shoots that are about four to five inches long and then cut them off the parent plant, just below a leaf node, with either a sharp knife or some clean garden scissors. You don't want a cutting with a flower bud on it as this will sap the plant's energy and it will not put down roots. Remove the bottom leaf growth so that you have a bare three-inch stem with a few leaves at the top. Dip the base of the stem into rooting hormone. This product comes in either liquid or powder form and protects the base of the cutting, while at the same time encouraging new roots to grow. I have no preference for either the powder or the liquid, but both have a shelf life, so check that whichever option you go for is in date.

I usually plant four to six cuttings around the edge of a four-inch pot filled with an even mixture of damp potting soil and perlite or vermiculite to promote drainage. Plant the cuttings two inches deep and then firm them in so that they are standing upright. Then cover the pot with a plastic bag, held in place with a rubber band. This creates a mini-greenhouse, which retains moisture and keeps up the humidity level.

Softwood cuttings should root in two to four weeks and hardwood cuttings in four to six weeks. Keep them on a warm windowsill until then and when you think they have rooted, you can remove the plastic bag and place them into a lightly sunny position. Let them become a little more established and then plant them into individual pots. The most common cause of death is overwatering. Let the top inch of soil dry out and only then water them using an organic liquid feed.

Figure 18. Lavender loving butterfly

As they become established, they can be moved into full sun and allowed to grow on until needed, or you can plant them into their final position. You can produce a large number of plants using this method and this can really save you a lot of money, especially if you are planting things like lavender hedges. A lavender hedge around the whole vegetable patch or even just a chosen bed is a powerful pest deterrent and can be very attractive to look at.

Allium tuberosum is commonly referred to under the name of either Chinese chives, wild onion or wild garlic. These plants originate from China, but are now frequently grown throughout the world as ornamental plants, favoured for their tiny white flowers, which make good cut flowers. Their edible leaves can be used for cooking and are a popular ingredient in herbal remedies and the flowers are often dried.

Figure 19. White blooming Chinese Chive

They are bulbous plants with strap-shaped leaves, which die back during the winter in all except the mildest of climates. Each spring, they reappear and gradually the clumps become bigger and bigger. These can be lifted from time to time and then divided, so that they can be replanted in positions more favourable to the gardener. When working with them, the gardener will quickly notice a strong, garlic-like smell and when planted among carrots, they act as a powerful deterrent for the pesky carrot fly. They do not do well when grown with alfalfa, as the plants compete with one another. If deer are a problem in your garden, then this plant is one that they will not be attracted to.

Propagation: Sow seeds in a tray in the spring and keep it in a cold frame until the seedlings are large enough to handle easily. At this stage, they can be pricked out and planted into pots. I would suggest planting two or three per pot so that they form small clumps. These clumps can be planted into the garden in autumn. They will retreat back into the soil over the winter, but will quickly re-emerge when the weather starts to improve and will flower profusely in mid-to-late summer. You will need to use fresh seed, as it does not store for more than a year, and once your plants are established, bunches should be lifted and divided every three years. You can gather your own seed towards the end of the flowering season simply by shaking out some of the black, triangular seed from the flower heads. It is a good idea to deadhead early, because these plants self-seed profusely and can leave you with a lot of weeding if they land where you don't want new plants. Once they are established, I don't bother growing from seed, but simply lift the clumps of bulbs, divide and replant each spring.

Crimson clover is a flowering plant with plenty of low-growing leaves, providing a wonderful habitat for hunting spiders. These spiders predate heavily on the caterpillars that are very fond of broccoli and therefore, this is another combination that you might want to consider. Crimson clover is frequently grown as a cover crop during the winter months, which can be dug into the bed as a green fertilizer come the spring.

Figure 20. Crimson flower looking radiant

Propagation: Sow seed in late summer. This allows young plants to become established before the really cold winter weather sets in. Sow into well-prepared soil and thin seedlings to three inches apart when they start to show their second set of leaves. If you live in a really cold area, you could hold back and sow plants in early spring. The plants will provide you with a carpet of one of the most attractive cover crops. Once the flowers go over and before they set seed, the plants can simply be sliced off at ground level using a hoe. They can then be dug into the bed to provide a green fertilizer that is high in nitrogen.

Artemisia absinthium is a grey-leafed plant with flat yellow flowers that is more commonly known as wormwood. It was once famed for its use in the production of a powerful alcohol spirit known as absinthe, which was eventually banned from much of Europe, because so many people were becoming alcoholics and going blind through its abuse. In the home garden, it is a great deterrent for carrot fly and can also be grown amongst onions, garlic and leeks. This plant can also be turned into a tea that has a powerful insecticidal property when sprayed on plants, but should only be used on ornamentals. Deer and rabbits don't like it, but will steal bites from crops in fairly close proximity.

Propagation: Although it is possible to grow this decid-uous perennial from seed, germination is slow and you would be well advised to opt for stem tip or heel cuttings, which take very easily. Stem tip cuttings are taken using the tops tips of the plant while they are still quite new. Cut off a three-inch stem tip of new growth in early to mid-summer, just below a leaf node. Remove the leaves on the lower two-thirds of your cutting, dip in hormone powder or solution and plant into a pot of ordinary potting soil. As with lavender, you can plant several cuttings in a pot and then pot them individually once rooting has taken place.

Figure 21. The yellow flower of Wormwood attracts beneficial insects

Heel cuttings are taken using slightly more mature plant material. Tear the cutting away from the parent plant, leaving a small heel where the cutting breaks away from the branch it was attached to. This heel is filled with nutrients that will provide the base from which new roots will soon shoot. Plant several of these heel cuttings in a pot and once they root, treat them as you would tip cuttings. It may seem quite a brutal approach to taking cuttings, but it won't harm the parent plant and is a very reliable method of propagating new plants. Once you pot up the seedlings, keep them in pots in a cold frame and plant them out the following spring. All artemisias are quite short-lived plants so it makes sense to grow new replacements on a regular basis.

Sage is a well-known culinary herb. It has attractive foliage with purple flower spikes and is extremely tolerant of harsh, dry conditions. Its odour is hated by many flying insects and particularly pests, although its rich blue flowers attract bees and other pollinators when the plant is flowering. It makes a good plant to grow beside tomatoes, carrots, thyme and rosemary. As well as being a good companion plant and useful culinary plant. There are over 800 different types of sage, ranging from bi-colour and tri-colour to deep purple, so you are spoiled for choice. Not all types are good for cooking, but they all provide an eye-catching groundcover. To keep this plant looking at its best, cut it back to two inches in early spring before new leaf growth begins. This will encourage the plant to put out more new shoots and leaves.

Figure 22. Sage is a fantastic culinary herb used in many Mediterranean dishes

Propagation: If you need lots of plants, then growing from seed may be your best option. Seeds need to undergo a period of cold to make them germinate well, so place your seed in a zip-lock bag with some sterilized sand and leave it in the fridge for a few weeks before sowing, which should take place in early spring. Sow four or five seeds into small pots filled with pre-dampened seed compost. Seed compost contains very few nutrients and is almost free of micro-organisms. This stops the soil from harbouring a disease called damping off disease, which many seedlings, including sage, are prone to. Lightly cover the seed with seed compost and then cover the pot with a sheet of glass or some clear plastic. Stand it on a windowsill or in a greenhouse at 10 to 15°C (50 – 59°F) and remove the plastic or glass for an hour per day to allow air to get in.

Seeds will germinate after two weeks and can be planted into individual containers once the second set of leaves appears. It will probably be eighteen months to two years before plants are strong enough to plant out, which is why I prefer to opt for cuttings. Patience is a great asset to successful gardening and a character trait which I am sadly lacking.

Take cuttings in mid-to-late summer. Cuttings should be around two-and-a-half inches in length from new growth at the crown of the plant. Remove most of the lower leaves, but leave at least three pairs remaining at the top of the cutting. Dip into hormone solution and plant three or four cuttings to a pot. These plants need to be kept moist and will take much better if they are kept humid. A simple way to do this is to create a cloche by cutting the base off a large clear plastic bottle and placing this over the top of the pot. Moisture build-up can be eliminated by simply unscrewing the lid of the bottle for an hour a day. Once the plants have rooted well, they can be placed into their own pots and kept moist, in a sunny position. They can be planted out the following spring.

Another easy way to start your cuttings is to simply start them off in a container of water. Stand your cuttings in a glass of water so that the bottom third remains permanently wet and stand the glass on a bright windowsill. This method is very easy but may not offer as high a success rate as planting into a soil mix. What is does offer is an easy way to see when the roots are becoming established enough to plant into pots.

Zinnia For years I wondered why so many people grew these delightful flowering plants alongside their vegetables. Because they are attractive and add a wide splash of colour, I had assumed that they were being grown as cut flowers and that some gardeners simply found it convenient to add them to the vegetable patch rather than into their ornamental beds. It turns out that Zinnias not only attract bees, but they are also favoured by many of the Japanese beetles that often become a pest on many crops.

When they are used for this purpose, they are being used as a trap crop. It is believed that they will be drawn to the flowers before the less showy vegetables. This makes catching the beetle quite easy, providing you check them regularly. However, if you fail to do that, then you will have the beetles move onto your crop within a few days.

Figure 23. Zinnia is one of the easiest annuals to grow

Propagation: These plants grow so easily that you can simply sow the seed directly into the ground. They should be blooming in sixty to seventy days. There is a huge range of varieties to choose from, which will offer different colours, sizes and forms. They come with single, semi-double and double blooms, as well as dwarf and tall varieties, so check the seed packet to be sure of planting distances. You will need to till the soil to a depth of eight inches, mix in a layer of compost and then you can start sowing in early spring, when the temperatures are starting to hit 15°C (60°F). Plant to a depth of a quarter inch and between fourteen and twenty-four inches apart, depending on which variety you opt for. In terms of their companion planting benefits, it will not make much difference which variety you opt for, so choose varieties that you like and experiment regularly.

It is a good idea to plant a succession of plants every week for a few weeks so that you are assured of an ongoing display of flowers throughout the summer.

Tansy was once very popular as a culinary herb, but seems to be used more as an ornamental these days. It is a tall plant with bright yellow flowers and a pungent odour that seems to deter ants, many species of beetle and some of the wasp species. It was once important for the dying of textiles. One of its major benefits is that it helps introduce potassium to the soil, which is a macronutrient that is needed by fruit and vegetable crops. For this reason, it is a great plant for adding to the compost heap. It is toxic to many animals and should not be cultivated in the vicinity of livestock.

Figure 24. The flowers of Tansy bloom in clusters and look like yellow buttons

Propagation: Tansy grows almost too easily and for this reason, I am a little hesitant in recommending it. Seeds are sown straight after the last frost and planted a quarter of an inch deep in just about any soil. When seedlings appear, thin them to one every six inches.

These perennials are extremely hardy and are regarded as an invasive noxious plant in some US states. Coming from the same family as the thistle, once established, they self-seed so profusely that you should never have to plant them again. They do require management in this regard, hence my reticence in recommending it as a companion plant. Though they need to be controlled carefully, they are a powerful weapon in the companion planting armory and one you will hear mentioned often. Deadhead regularly and dig out and compost seedlings before they become established and you should be able to keep them in check.

Cosmos One of the reasons these plants are so frequently used as companion plants is that they are so easy to grow. Seed can be sown directly and they require little more attention than an occasional watering, which you can combine with your regular watering schedule. They come in a wide range of heights and colours and are highly favoured by lacewings, especially if they have orange flowers. The delicate lacewing may be a fragile-looking creature, but they are voracious eaters of aphids and other soft-bodied pests.

Figure 25. The frilly texture of the Cosmos bloom

Propagation: These stunning plants are easy to grow and can be sown directly into the bed or started off in pots. From sowing to the arrival of the first flowers can take as long as seven weeks, so the main incentive for starting them in pots is to bring forward that first flower flush. The range of colours is enormous, as is the difference in height, so you will be spoiled for choice.

If you are going to plant them directly into the ground, dig the earth but don't enrich it too much. If these plants are too well fed, they will produce an abundance of foliage at the expense of the flowers that you are after. Sow seed a quarter of an inch deep and twelve to eighteen inches apart, depending on the variety you have chosen. If you want to start them off earlier, plant them into trays of seed compost five weeks before the last frosts are expected. They can be potted into larger individual pots of general-purpose compost when they are large enough to handle and planted into their final position soon after the risk of frost has passed.

They will continue to produce flowers over a much longer period if you deadhead regularly and will last for days in a vase of water when used as cut flowers. They are very drought-tolerant and need little in the way of additional feeding. The one downside is that they do self-seed prolifically and if you don't want them growing abundantly in the same place the following year, you will need to cut off heads before they set seed. Seeds can be collected and replanted. One easy way to collect seed without it being widely dispersed is to place paper bags over chosen blooms just before they set seed and holding them in place with elastic bands. The seeds can be shaken off into the bags when ripe.

Sunflowers, as we have seen in the 'Three Sisters' example, are a classic support plant for things like climbing beans. They don't get on well with potatoes, as their roots, which spread quite widely, secrete toxins that potatoes don't like. They are equally valuable for their ability to attract both honey and bumblebees, as well as many seed-eating birds. There might not seem to be much advantage to having seed-eaters in your garden.

What few people realise is that these seed-eaters become voracious insectivores during the nesting season.

Figure 26. Bird feasting on Sunflower

Tits will lay between seven and fourteen eggs per brood and can have as many as three broods per season. Parents will feed their young on caterpillars and other insects, such as aphids, and will bring food back to the nest as many as seven hundred times per day. I can think of few examples of how the relationship between the gardener and nature is better exemplified. Imagine the advantages of having just two or three pairs breeding near your garden. Growing sunflowers will encourage this.

Even outside of the breeding season, these birds continue to supplement their diet with the odd insect, so offering them any reason to move into your garden has obvious benefits. Once established, they never move more than twenty miles from home. In addition to the sunflowers, I supply breeding boxes and supplementary seed throughout the year, and the increase in the number of birds has been quite dramatic.

Propagation: This is another plant that is often given to kids to plant, because it is so easy to grow and can yield such spectacular results. Many people think of sunflowers purely in terms of the large yellow variety we see growing in agricultural fields. In fact, the range of both colours and sizes is quite extraordinary. If you are looking for more of a companion plant than an ornamental, then choose a variety that will produce seed and a strong stem to climb. Pure flowering varieties may attract insects, but they will not lure in the army of insect-eating birds that can be so useful for eliminating caterpillars.

You can plant them directly into your garden as soon as the last frosts have passed. Sow them into well-cultivated soil at a depth of one to two inches and at a distance of six inches apart. They are not heavy feeders and do not need a very rich soil. Water them in and make sure that the soil doesn't dry out completely. They should start appearing in seven days and can be thinned out to two feet when the first true leaves are established. It is advisable to stake taller varieties, though they are pretty robust.

Nepeta is more commonly referred to by the common name of catnip. It produces an oil known as nepetalactone, which many cats find highly addictive, and unless you grow your plants in a sheltered area, you may find them being crushed by cats, which love to roll in their leaves.

This plant is extremely hardy and will thrive on even the poorest of soils. It has quite pungent leaves that repel many insects and flowers which bees delight in visiting. It makes a good companion plant for pumpkins, beetroot and squash. When growing at its peak, this plant can be extremely attractive and provides a very thick groundcover, supporting deep purple flowers. The problem is that if left unattended, it tends to spread too widely and becomes straggly and scruffy looking. The easiest way to deal with this is to cut back hard with a pair of hedge clippers immediately after flowering. You can be quite ruthless in this regard, as the plant will soon recover and will be flowering again within a matter of weeks.

Figure 27. *Nepeta Faassenii* "Six Heels giant"

Seed can be directly sown outdoors either in spring or early autumn. The seed casings themselves are quite hard and you will need to stratify them before sowing. The easiest way to do this is to place them in a plastic bag in the freezer for twenty-four hours and then soak them overnight in warm water. This softens the outer layer of the seed, allowing moisture to penetrate and facilitating easier and much more reliable germination. Many nurseries will sell potted plants, if you don't wish to propagate yourself. They thrive in full sun and need little in the way of feeding. I find this a useful plant to grow along the edge of beds as it defines borders, whilst at the same time, providing a pest repellent that is really attractive to bees.

Sweet peas should not be confused with edible peas, but the two plants grow very well in combination with one another. The sweet pea produces very fragrant flowers, which offer an incentive for pollinators to move in. They are part of the leguminous family, meaning that they help in binding nitrogen, which is always advantageous. I must confess that part of the reason I like having them in my garden is the scent that they reward me with when I am working nearby. I am not sure that this necessarily qualifies them as good companion plants but I am willing to pretend that it does.

Propagation: Sweet peas can be bought as plugs, but they should really be grown from seed for best results and most value for money. Sow them indoors in March, but before doing so, soak the seeds overnight. Doing this will cause them to absorb moisture through their tough husks and they will swell up and take far more readily than if planted dry.

Figure 28. *Lathyrus Latifolius* pea blossom

They are deep-rooted plants, so choose tall pots and sow five seeds to a pot. Choose a good compost and make sure that is always damp. The seeds should be sown to a depth of half an inch and gently firmed down. Keep them indoors or in a greenhouse until April, when there is little chance of frost. They ae very vulnerable to slugs and snails at this fragile stage in their lives, so you will need to take precautions in this regard. When they are six inches tall, they will start to look a bit leggy and you can cut them back to just above a leaf node to encourage them to bush out. That will produce more stems and more stems mean more flowers.

Harden them off for a week before planting them to their final position. They will need a support to grow up and I usually make one by just driving some canes into the bed and tying the tops together to form a sort of wigwam or pyramid shape. These guys are heavy feeders, so make sure that the soil you plant them into is rich in compost and give a liquid feed at least once a fortnight. Place two or three of your seedlings in each planting hole and plant them about six inches apart.

They climb using tendrils, but tend only to have a vague sense of discipline in this regard. Once a week, you should gently tie them into the climbing frame using soft twine, to keep them growing vertically. Towards the end of summer, they will start producing seed prolifically at the expense of the flowers that you are after. This can be controlled by regular harvesting of the flowers, which will cause a much longer flush. Cut off all of the flowers and keep just the forming buds at least once a week. They are wonderful as cut flowers in vases.

Alyssum is a low-growing flowering plant that produces mounds of attractive white flowers that bees find irresistible, as do some beneficial wasp species. They are frequently grown along the edge of beds and borders in the ornamental garden because they provide such a stunning display, but they also make for useful companion plants in the vegetable garden.

Technically, these are perennials which should retreat into the soil in the winter and reappear in the spring. Most gardeners tend to treat them as annuals and this is what I would recommend. After the last of the frosts have passed, prepare your soil by raking it to a light tilth, then spread the fine seed by rubbing it between thumb and forefinger. Rake again lightly to ensure an even spread and then water in with a fine spray.

Figure 29. Sweet carpet of snow

You should have decent sized plants in thirty to forty days. They prefer cooler weather, so what often happens is that they fade when it gets hot and then reappear in the autumn with a second flush of bloom. They self-seed very easily, so you should keep having flowers year after year. Although most commonly seen in their white form, there are pastel pinks and purples as well.

You now have a substantial list of flowering plants that you can use in your companion planting communities, as well as the ability to grow them yourself. It is by no means a definitive guide, but it is wide enough for you to always have some form of plant with which to create beneficial plant combinations. Over time, you will discover more, either through trial and error or from listening to what the local gardeners in your area are using. Very often gardeners will be using odd combinations that may only be relevant in a particular area or circumstance. Just because they haven't made it onto this list doesn't mean that the combination is not valid. Be prepared to experiment widely for the best results.

4

THE VEGETABLE GARDEN

For the determined home grower, the vegetable patch is the engine room of the garden. As you will see later in this book, it is far from the only area where different plants can be combined to achieve various benefits. It is, however, probably the area where people are most familiar with the concept of companion planting. In this chapter, we will focus on the vegetable garden and work our way through some of the most commonly grown vegetables and some of the many plant combinations with which they can be grown.

It would be impossible to cover all the combinations, because some of these are subjective and some plant communities might be relevant in one area but might serve no purpose in another. There is little point, for example, in growing plants to protect against Japanese beetle where there aren't any and where the main threat is from aphids. I will show you some of the main companion planting options, but you are now able to mix and match using the information in the previous chapters. Hopefully what happens here builds on that.

Asparagus: asparagus is quite unusual in the edible garden in that it is a hardy perennial. It appears each spring and then retreats back into the earth just before winter, only to re-emerge the following spring. It will take you three years before you're getting a full harvest off the plant, but thereafter that you can look forward to between ten and fifteen years of regular, delicious asparagus spikes. Production will start to decrease in the last five years, but will still be fairly plentiful. It is a good idea to start bringing on replacement plants when your plants are seven to eight years old.

Figure 30. Ready to harvest green Asparagus

This plant partners well with a large number of plants, but is most famous for pairing with tomatoes. This is for a very simple reason: tomatoes emit a chemical known as solanine, which drives away the major threat to asparagus, the asparagus beetle. Both parsley and basil do the same thing and, as they enhance the flavour of the tomato, you're looking at a great four-way combination.

Although asparagus is quite easy going and partners well with most plants, don't attempt to grow garlic, onions or potatoes nearby as they simply don't get on with one another.

Beans: Beans are divided into two categories—bush beans and climbing beans.

First, we will look at bush beans and here we will include butter beans, snap beans and string beans.

All of these combine well with cucumbers and corn. They are happy with most brassicas, as well as tomatoes, eggplants (aubergines) and potatoes. Never plant them with fennel or onions.

Climbing beans are happiest with corn, peas, chard, eggplants and radishes. Like the bush bean, they don't like to be with onions or fennel, nor are they too fond of leeks. They stunt the growth of beets.

Beets: Beets are one of the easiest garden vegetables to grow. They are not prone to very many pests or diseases, don't take up much space and companion well with a wide range of other vegetables and herbs. They are quite tolerant of cold weather, which means you can get them into the ground early in the spring. In addition, they are a versatile vegetable and there are dozens of different ways in

Figure 31. Outdoor permaculture garden with companion planting of Corn and Green beans plants

which they can be prepared or stored. Don't just eat the root. The leaves are edible too and make a colourful addition to salads that is both heathy and tasty.

They are members of the Swiss chard family and though chard is grown for its leaves, beets are grown for their bulbous root. Like many root vegetables, they should be sown directly into the garden, because they do not transplant well. It is also a good idea to soften your seed by soaking it overnight before planting. It likes quite a rich soil, so if you know that your soil is lacking in nutrients, it should be beefed up prior to sowing.

Figure 32. The Beatroots garden

Plant your beets with bush beans, butter beans, cauliflower, broccoli, kale and of course Swiss chard. A particularly good partnership is beets and lettuce. Lettuce offers weed-suppression benefits, and its roots shallower than those of the beets, meaning that the two plants can be sown quite close together. Another good pairing is between beets and radishes. At first this might not seem like a good idea, because they are both root vegetables, but in fact, radishes grow far more quickly and so their roots open and prepare the soil. They are harvested before they are likely come into competition with the beets, so the combination works well.

About the only plant you don't want to plant beets with is pole/climbing beans, as they do not perform well together.

Broccoli: Broccoli is one of the most nutritious of garden vegetables. Although tolerant of most soils, broccoli is a heavy feeder, so unless your soil is already rich, you will be well-advised to beef it up with a high-nitrogen product, such as well-rotted garden manure, prior to planting.

This plant is prone to a number of pests, such as cabbage butterfly, cabbage root fly and some of the beetle family. For this reason, having some fragrant herbs in the area makes a lot of sense. Try lemon balm, lemongrass, basil, rosemary or oregano.

The plant pairs well with celery, onions, garlic, shallots, leeks, potatoes and bush beans. It does not, however, pair well with its relatives from the brassica family, simply because they too are heavy feeders and when grown in proximity to one another, they compete for the same nutrients.

Figure 33. A growing Broccoli flower head

For some reason, this plant does not pair well with members of the nightshade family, so don't try to grow it with tomatoes, hot peppers or eggplant.

Cabbage: Cabbage is a member of the brassica family, which includes cauliflower, bok/pak choi, mustard, broccoli and Brussels sprouts, among many others. Many of these are very popular in the vegetable garden and they are often threatened by the same pests. This means that the companion plants that you select for one member of this family will also protect the others.

One common threat here comes from the cabbage white caterpillar. The butterfly itself poses no risk, and is even useful as a pollinator. It is the caterpillar that can so quickly decimate your produce. The butterfly lays her pale eggs on the underside of leaves and as soon as they hatch, her offspring start to eat whatever plant they happen to find themselves on. They are amazingly well camouflaged and it is really easy not to notice them for a day or two, by which time they have grown much larger and a large population of them can decimate an immature cabbage overnight. The worst thing is that there is no such thing as one colony of caterpillars. One day you are happily admiring your crop and the next you have an invasion of these creatures in what will feel like plague proportions. The fact of the matter is that they were there earlier, but you just failed to notice them. It is one reason why a good gardener must always pay close attention to his plants. Very often, disaster can be avoided by simply looking under the leaves of some of the plants on a daily basis.

Eggs and even young caterpillars can be dealt with quite easily. That changes once they become large and established.

Figure 34. Marigolds deters cabbageworms and add bright color to the garden

These are thirsty plants that should be planted alongside other plants that also need plenty of water. They also prefer a soil that is rich in nutrients. Borage and buckwheat both help to draw minerals to the surface of the soil, where they can be accessed by your cabbages. Borage also seems to deter the cabbage white butterfly. Onions and marjoram deter both the cabbage white and cabbage worm. Cabbage can be grown alongside most aromatics, with the most notable being rosemary, dill and marjoram, and some gardeners will swear that marjoram actually improves the taste of cabbage.

Radishes don't combine well with cabbage and strawberries are notorious for attracting slugs and snails, so that is another combination to avoid.

Carrots: Carrots are a popular vegetable with the home grower and they are generally quite gregarious, with the exception of dill, with which they should never be planted. The one pest that really troubles carrot growers is the carrot fly. These tiny creatures lay their eggs low on the leaf of the carrot and when they hatch, the grubs crawl down and start munching on the root below the soil. Often the gardener does not become aware that the crop is under attack until it is too late to do anything about it. Carrot flies locate their target plant through odour, so if we can disguise that odour, we stand a very good chance of eliminating or reducing these attacks. Here the obvious partners are plants with a strong smell of their own, such as onions, garlic and leeks, as well as aromatics such as sage, rosemary and wormwood.

Carrots pair well with lettuce, tomatoes, chives and leeks. The carrot-tomato combination is one I find very useful. Tomatoes produce a natural insect-deterrent called solanine and provide some dappled shade, while the carrot opens up the soil and allows water and air to permeate more freely.

Figure 35. Onions reduce carrot flies attacks

Leeks deter carrot fly and carrots deter leek moth and onion fly, so that is another reciprocal arrangement you might want to consider when putting together your planting plan.

Cucumbers: Another useful salad crop, cucumbers do best when allowed to climb, and corn is an ideal combination for this. Their main pests are rust fly and cucumber beetle and both of these creatures are deterred by the presence of radishes, so that makes for a useful pairing. It is a good idea to plant a few radishes at the base of your cucumber vine and then just allow them to complete their lifecycle without pulling them.

This makes them sacrificial plants, but as these plants grow so easily, it makes sense to lose a few of them in order to have healthier cucumbers. Cucumbers also pair well with peas, beans celery and carrots. Don't grow them anywhere near potatoes, as they can introduce phytoph-thora blight, to which the

Image 36. Climbing cucumber vine plant

potato is susceptible. Also, don't pair them with basil, sage or cauliflower.

Leeks: This plant grows well when planted alongside any of its cousins, such as onions, shallots or garlic. It is also perfectly happy alongside beets, celery, spinach and particularly carrots. When grown with carrots, leeks help to repel carrot fly, while the carrots are a deterrent to onion fly, so it is easy to see how this plant combination has much to offer. In addition, when grown near to one another, they both break up the soil, allowing the roots to penetrate more easily.

Figure 37. Leek vegetable harvest

Although leeks should be planted out after the last frosts have past, they will tolerate light frosts when they are young and when mature in the autumn they will even tolerate quite heavy frosts. It is tempting to plant leeks quite close together, because they take up very little space, but you should be aware that the closer they are planted to one another, the smaller they will be. This may work well for you if you like small, tender plants, but commercial growers tend to grow them six to eight inches apart to maximize their size. Many people chop off the green top leaves and simply eat the white part of this vegetable. The green leaves are tough, but break down nicely when boiled and make an excellent addition to soups and stews.

These plants do not like to be planted alongside hot peppers, pole/climbing beans, or peas.

Lettuce: This is a widely consumed crop that is almost essential to any summer salad bowl. Lettuces prefer to be kept slightly cool and their leaves make them a big favourite with both slugs and snails.

Figure 38. Your very own spring mixed garden salad

Mint can be a useful deterrent for these pests. The plants are also vulnerable to aphids, so think about growing them with strongly scented crops such as chives and garlic. Marigolds are also good at deterring aphids, although, with lettuce, you would be better off with one of the more compact French varieties, rather than their taller African cousins.

They will grow happily alongside beans, broccoli and beets, as well as cucumbers.

Onions: I have already mentioned onions on several occasions, as they are so useful for deterring various pests such as carrot fly on other plants. They are vulnerable to a pest of their own, and that is the maggot of the onion fly. One handy trick for reducing the risk of maggots is not to plant your onions in rows. The maggots move from plant to plant and our long-standing tradition of lining this crop in neat orderly rows has played very much to their advantage. If you dot your onions throughout the garden, you stand a better chance of harvesting a healthy crop.

They will grow well with many different plants and this makes random planting more viable. They do particularly well when grown alongside brassicas and offer them protection as we have seen above. They are equally happy when grown among beets, lettuce or tomatoes. Don't grow them in close proximity to beans and peas.

Figure 39. Lettuce and onions are an example of great companion plants

Our obsession with growing things in neat rows has played into the hands (mandibles?) of many of the most common pests in our gardens. Mass planting is not in accordance with the way that plants would grow in a more natural environment and we have unwittingly created a problem for ourselves. It is one that our obsessively orderly minds are strangely reluctant to free themselves from. This is gradually being readdressed as people start to become more at home with the concept of permaculture gardening, which is starting to gain a toehold in the modern gardener's psyche. We will look at this more natural method of gardening later in the series, when we deal with the vegetable garden.

Parsnips: These root vegetables seemed to go out of fashion a decade or so ago, but have made a strong comeback in recent years.

They're quite easy-going in terms of who they will companion with, but there one or two minor tricks you will need to master if you're going to cultivate them successfully. For starters, always grow them using fresh seed, as the seed does not store well. They require a long growing period and need a touch of frost before they are harvested. Some gardeners will even leave them in the ground over the winter months, although if you want to do this you need to cover them with a thick bed of mulch before the winter really sets in.

Figure 40. In the associated crop garden - row of parsnips surrounded by carrots, in front of a row of white borage

As soon as the ground is workable, dig in compost or broken-down manure to depth of between twelve and fifteen inches. Rake it over and plant your seeds at a depth of half an inch and at two-inch intervals. It is a good idea to plant two seeds per hole. After two to three weeks, your plants will start to appear and you can thin them to between three and six inches apart. One trick that is quite commonly used when growing plants in stony ground is to place the cardboard inner of a toilet roll into the soil, fill it with soil and drop the seeds into that. This will ensure that the root of the plant can reach a reasonable size without hitting a stone and distorting. The cardboard gradually breaks down and by the time it does, the parsnip is large enough to push any more stones out of the way.

Main threats come from aphids, leaf miners and carrot fly and as you will know, these can be deterred by inter-planting with garlic, or onions. Parsnips also grow quite happily with radishes, peppers, bush beans and peas. They are sometimes attacked by root maggots and these are difficult pests to deter with companion planting. Sprinkle fire ash around your plants and that should prevent this problem occurring.

Potatoes: Potatoes have a number of plants that they will grow alongside quite happily. Don't plant them with other members of the nightshade family, because they have similar nutritional requirements and both plants are likely to suffer. This means keeping them away from tomatoes, peppers and eggplants/aubergines.

Figure 41. Marigold protecting potatoes

Potatoes are susceptible to blight and plants that could introduce this problem include cucumbers, squash, tomatoes and raspberries. Also, they will not thrive alongside brassicas, carrots, parsnips or asparagus.

Good companions include bush beans, garlic, peas, celery and marigolds.

Pumpkin: I think there can be few people who don't love that splash of orange colour that pumpkins provide in the autumn. In the kitchen, they offer many advantages, because, provided they are stored carefully, they will keep for almost the whole of winter. That provides a wonderful fresh vegetable to add to stews and soups at a time when there are not many other vegetables around. They can also be delicious when made into pies and jams, which is something some gardeners tend to overlook. When storing these vegetables, place them in a cool, shady environment, such as a garden shed or garage. Take great care not to bruise them, as this will allow rot to set in; stand them on a bed of dry straw. Pumpkins are susceptible to quite an array of pests, including cucumber beetle, aphids and a number of different borers.

For this reason, it makes sense to grow them with aromatics, including many herbs or flowers, such as nasturtiums. It is also widely believed that when grown with marjoram, the taste of the pumpkin is enhanced.

One of the most widely talked about plant combinations is that of The Three Sisters, which we mentioned right at the beginning of this book. That consists of corn, pole beans and pumpkin, where the corn acts as a trellis for the beans, the beans trap nitrogen for the pumpkin and the pumpkin provides a weed-suppressing mulch. Pumpkins are heavy feeders, which is not surprising when you see how far they can spread their trailing stems and leaves. For this reason, your nitrogen fixing plants such as beans and peas make good companion plants.

Pumpkins don't seem to like being grown with pota-toes, but other than that, are fairly easy growing, though you must bear in mind that their rampant spread might suffocate smaller plants.

Tomatoes: I have heard it said that a vegetable garden is not a vegetable garden without tomatoes growing somewhere. Fortunately, they are quite sociable plants and many of the combinations

Figure 42. The Three Sister planting method

available are said to improve flavour as well as to develop health and vigor.

The combination that you are most likely to hear about is that of tomatoes and basil. In my experience, it is one of the most widely touted combinations in the companion gardening arena. Not only does the basil improve the taste of the tomato, whilst benefitting from the shade of the tomato leaves, but basil also reduces blight, from which tomatoes often suffer. Borage attracts beneficial insects and draws up nutrients, while deterring tomato horn beetle. Garlic reduces blight and aphids, but particularly red spider mite, which can become a problem in some gardens.

Figure 43. Genova Basil is believed to improve the flavor of its companion Tomato plant

Other plants that will grow happily alongside tomatoes are peas, lettuce, mint and lemon balm. Nasturtiums and marigolds are commonly seen in tomato beds, because of their insect repellant properties.

Don't plant them alongside cabbage, fennel or broccoli. I try to separate them from all members of the brassica family, as well as potatoes.

Radishes: Small, reliable and quick to produce a crop, the radish is one of the first plants to sow in the vegetable garden in spring. They grow well with beets, carrots, cucumbers melons and squash. Many beetles find them repellant, which makes them fine companions for plants that are commonly attacked by different varieties of these pests, such as cucumber and melons.

Because of the fact that they grow fast and take up little space, they make a great little plant for intercropping with many different vegetables. They can be dotted between carrots or parsnips, thus loosening the ground a little, and will still be harvested in time to allow the carrots to reach full size. Because we gardeners now have access to varieties that will produce much later in the season, it is a good idea to hold stock of different seed types that will allow for a succession of planting and harvesting times. That means every time you have a bit of a gap in a bed, you can pop in a few seeds, which will soon reach maturity.

Figure 44. Root earth agriculture

About the only plants with which you should not consider combining radishes are the brassica family. Radishes might attract flea beetle, which will happily spread to plants such as cabbages or Brussels sprouts.

Zucchini: These plants are known as courgettes in Europe. They are normally eaten when they are about six inches long, though the fruit can be allowed to grow much larger, when it is often referred to as a marrow. In both Italy and France, the flowers are often stuffed with mince and herbs and eaten as a delicacy.

Figure 45. Courgette and Beans growing under
the sun rays

This is an easy-going plant that partners well with beans, corn, peas and spinach, as well as many herbs, including oregano and dill. Bear in mind that this plant can grow quite large and the broad leaves can easily spread over nearly a square yard. It requires rich soil and plenty of water. When watering, try not to get water onto the leaves; instead, aim for the base of the plant as they can be prone to mildew and other fungal problems. Do not grow this plant with either potatoes or pumpkin.

5

THE ORCHARD

So far, we have mainly focused on companion plants that are used in the vegetable garden, but fruit trees can also benefit from community planting. Very often, the same companion plants can be used, but people simply don't know what to plant with their fruit trees, or they simply don't think of combining plant companions with trees. Garlic, for example, deters the green peach aphid and growing a few of these plants beneath peach or nectarine trees can really boost your crop. Likewise, basil is an aromatic herb which seems to increase the productivity of apricot trees, due to the fact that it deters pests. In return, the tree provides dappled shade, which basil thrives in.

Nearly all of the beneficial flowering plants we have just looked at can have positive effects when grown beneath fruit trees. Not only do they act as insect deterrents and attract pollinators, but many of them also create a sort of living mulch that inhibits weed growth and helps to retain moisture. Plants such as comfrey, with its deep rooting system, helps to draw nutrients up through the soil structure to where they become more available to your fruiting plant. Just be careful, because comfrey can spread like wildfire and is hard to get under control of once it has got a grip.

Figure 46. Bumblebee collecting the pollen from
an apple blossom

There is another factor that comes into play when you have an orchard. Some fruit trees will not set fruit if they are not pollinated from the flowers of another tree. This means that having the right companions nearby is not just a luxury: it is imperative if you are going to have fruit. Likewise, the pollination process is often carried out by insects carrying pollen from one tree to another. Those insects need to be nurtured, especially as we are seeing such massive declines in the insect population at the moment. In parts of China, the decline is so acute that people are being paid to hand pollinate the cherry trees—a job that was once carried out far more effectively, and for free, by naturally occurring insects.

Apple The apple tree is probably one of the most quintessential of all fruit trees. One of the wonders about modern cultivars is that breeders have been able to come up with varieties of many different sizes, meaning that you don't necessarily need a huge garden in order to grow your own apples. Most apples benefit from having another apple tree in near proximity in order to pollinate fully and produce a good harvest. Breeders have also been able to make adaptions in that regard and some trees are able to pollinate themselves or have had a branch from another tree grafted into them, which is sufficient for pollination to take place.

Not all apples are compatible and it is always worth speaking to a nursery that specialises in fruit trees if you are unsure what to plant. You will be amazed at the choices available and the knowledge that these people have. You will be able to choose a tree not only in relation to its size, but also to the type of fruit that most suits your personal taste. Espaliers can be grown as fans on walls or be trained as low growing stepovers on the perimeters of your other beds.

Figure 47. Red juicy apples are a treat for the eyes and the taste buds

Apple tree roots grow down deep and send out radial roots horizontally, which suck up nutrients and water. In just three years, an apple tree's combined root system can total over a mile in length if it were to be laid end to end. Luckily, they are not destructive like the roots of some trees, so they can be planted close to walls without fear of damage. Many of the radial roots might be quite shallow and therefore suffer from competition from grasses with their thickly matted root systems.

Good companion plants that can help address this problem include garlic, onions and leeks. Chives help to prevent apple scab and also deter rabbits if that is one of the pests that you have to contend with. One of my favorite plants to combine with apple trees is white clover. Not only do its flowers attract beneficial insects, but it also fixes nitrogen and offers a pleasing visual effect.

Quince In my opinion, the quince tree is one of the most under-utilized of fruit trees. It is closely related to the apple and is believed by many historians to have been the original fruit of temptation that was mentioned in the book of Genesis. Many apples are grown on quince rootstock. The trees are normally smaller than apple trees and offer a pleasing appearance and wonderful-smelling blossoms.

The reason that so little attention is given to these trees is that their fruit cannot simply be plucked from the tree and eaten raw in the same way that an apple can. With a little effort and only the vaguest degree of culinary skill, they can be turned into delicious jams and jellies or simply tossed in with a pork roast and treated a bit like a potato.

If preparing fruit in this way seems like too much effort, then you might want to consider just growing them as an ornamental in the flower garden. With some light pruning, they can be trained into a lovely shape; they don't get overly large and that scent makes them an excellent choice, even if you simply compost the fruit or give it away.

Whether you choose to grow them for their fruit or as a landscape focal point, they are happiest when grown along with borage, chives, marigolds, comfrey or dill. We will revisit these trees in more details later in the book, when we delve more deeply into ornamental companion planting.

Figure 48. Bright golden yellow Quince fruit

Cherries Cherry trees are longstanding favourites in both the ornamental and fruit garden. Edible cherries can be divided into two categories—sweet cherries and sour cherries. Sweet cherries are what most people are probably most familiar with and they are one of those fruits that are highly sought after during the all too short fruiting season. Sour cherries need to have some sort of culinary magic applied to them to transform them from something sour and inedible into something sweet and delicious. In addition, there are many types of flowering cherries that are grown just for that brief but memorable flush of blossom that the Japanese have so successfully turned into a tourist attraction in its own right.

Figure 48. Stunning Japanese cherry blossom tree

Figs Fig trees can be one of the most reliable fruit trees in your garden. Man has been cultivating this tree for at least 10,000 years, so we have a long history of supporting one another. They do have an extensive root system and it is important to choose your planting position carefully because they can cause damage to foundations and walls.

When first planted, it is beneficial to contain the roots, as this encourages the tree to produce fruit earlier in its life. In the Victorian era, it was common to plant the tree in an old suitcase or travelling bag. They will, of course, break out eventually, but it speeds fruit production in younger trees.

Rue is a common companion plant and it originates from the same region as the fig, so the two have probably been growing side by side since well before they were both cultivated. The grey-leafed rue produces yellow flowers that deter fruit flies. The fruit on these trees tends to soften quite quickly, so fruit flies love them.

Another plant that will thrive under the fig is the common nettle. Nettles bind nitrogen and their flowers attract insect-eating pests. Of course, they do come with one major disadvantage in that they sting like hell and this is going to make accessing the fruit difficult. As soon as I can see the fruit ripening, I cut down all of the nettles with long-handled clippers. You can use a strimmer to achieve a faster result, but the flying debris will sting you if you don't wear tough trousers and a visor. Once cut, rake up the nettles and then either toss them into a drum of water for a fortnight to make nettle tea or add them to the compost heap. They are very high in nutrients, so your garden will love them.

Diluted, nettle tea makes a wonderful natural insecticide against aphids and caterpillars, but here you need to be aware of another disadvantage. Nettle tea smells. I am not talking about a vaguely unpleasant odor. I am talking about a smell that is so noxious that even your dog won't want to have anything to do with you if it blows onto your skin or clothes. You need to make sure which way the wind is blowing before squirting this product around. Other than that, it is great.

Figure 49. Nettle plant known for its stinging leaves

Marigolds will deter eelworm, which may be an issue with young trees, and comfrey draws up nutrients. In both of these cases, once the tree's root system is established, it will be able to fend for itself.

Rhododendrons are sometimes planted beneath fig trees and this has become somewhat controversial in gardening circles of late. Fig trees are deep-rooted, while rhododendrons are shallow-rooted, so one can see a correspondence there. Also, rhododendrons like dappled shade and the fig will certainly provide that. In my opinion, that is where the advantages end. As soon as the rhododendron becomes large, it makes accessing the fruit really difficult and this outweighs any advantage that may be offered to the fig tree. If you want great rhododendrons, then fine, but don't combine them if you are after plenty of figs.

Citrus If you are lucky enough to live an area where citrus can be grown outdoors, then you gain access to a plethora of fruit that is both nice to eat and rich in vitamins.

Figure 50. Lemon trees make a great stand alone feature for your patio

Citruses are, however, sometimes prone to insect pests. As usual in cases where pests are a possibility, borage and marigolds can attract predatory insects and deter some of the pests. Nasturtiums can be grown as a sacrificial plant to draw away the attention of aphids.

Herbs often combine well with citrus and they provide a great culinary reward as well as attracting predators. Try dill, fennel and yarrow and once the trees become established enough to cast some shade, then add basil.

If you have a problem with caterpillars, lemon balm or tansy should be considered, as they attract the caterpillar-eating tachinid fly.

Peas will bind nitrogen and provide you with some edible benefits and they grow quite happily near all types of citrus fruit.

Pears The pear tree is probably second to the apple when it comes to popularity in the orchard or garden. The trees bear many similarities in their cultivation requirements, including the fact that they are both self-sterile and so you will probably need a tree of a different variety to be growing nearby if you are going to get fruit.

Clover, nasturtiums and marigolds will all help with pest control, while peas and beans will lock in nitrogen and yield an edible harvest. An unusual companion plant used by some gardeners is the foxglove, which is believed to prolong the fruit after they are picked.

Figure 51. Foxglove is an interesting companion plant for your orchard

Walnuts The black walnut is a tree you might see growing in some orchards. They are large trees that can become enormous and besides their nuts, the timber they produce is of great value.

Figure 52. Fresh green Walnuts

The nuts are currently being used for experiments for their medicinal properties and many who eat them claim that they are a superfood.

Many of the more mature trees growing in older gardens may have originally been planted with their timber in mind. Even the hulls that encase the nuts can be ground up to produce a dye that is often used as a wood stain. If you have ever gathered walnuts you will quickly have learned that the hulls can stain your hands to the point you look like the world's worst chain smoker and that the discolouration takes several days to fade.

While they can be striking trees that produce great tasting and healthy nuts, they come with their own very specific set of considerations. They produce a chemical known as juglone from both their leaves and their roots. The chemical is designed to eliminate competition from other plants growing nearby and it is pretty effective at doing its job.

Many of the plants that you attempt to grow under or near to a walnut will fail simply because of the effects this chemical has. I would recommend that you don't try to grow any vegetable within fifty feet of one unless it is in a raised bed and clear of the tree's drip line. There are trees that will tolerate growing near to walnuts and these include black cherries, apples, pears and plums.

Plums When growing plums in an orchard, the conditions also tend to include damsons and greengages. These trees are regarded as being among the lower-maintenance trees to have in your garden. Once they are established, they ask for very little and still seem to provide bumper yields year after year.

One of the most common threats they face is from aphids, with both the leaf curling and mealy aphid as possible culprits. In terms of companion planting, the plants you choose will be the same. You want to attract aphid predators, such as lacewings, ladybirds and earwigs. Marigolds, nasturtiums and lavender are all common favourites, but herbs such as chives, comfrey, dill and lavender are also recommended. Plant them close to the tree, but leave room so that you can collect the fruit.

Peaches can be wonderful trees, but they are susceptible to some pests and health problems.

Many of these can be eliminated using correct pruning techniques, but there is certainly an argument to made for growing companion plants alongside them.

Tansy increases the potassium levels in the soil, which is the macronutrient that is often in short supply with many of the fruit-bearing

Figure 53. Ready to pick ripe Peach fruit

trees. Garlic helps with wood borer. This pest is often associated with these trees and they thrive beneath its bark. We have also already seen that garlic acts as a deterrent for another common pest—the aphid. Peach trees are quite susceptible to fungal disease and again, garlic can be of use here.

Harmful nematodes are put off by the presence of marigolds, while basil drives away thrips and at the same time benefits from the shade offered by the peach tree. Many gardeners report that when basil is grown beneath peach trees, the flavour of the fruit is enhanced.

Cane fruit is normally easy-going but can be susceptible to the occasional visits from passing pests, which include ants and Japanese beetles. Yarrow, tansy and chervil will all be of benefit here. For some reason that we don't understand, gooseberries seem to be happiest when growing in the vicinity of blackcurrants.

There have been few scientific studies done on many of these suggestions and much of what we know about the benefits of combining fruit and companion plants comes down to folklore, trial-and-error and common sense, once we have a greater understanding of what the major companion plants are effective against.

Figure 54. Companion Planting of Fruit Trees, Flowers and
Home Grown Organic Vegetables

6

HERBS

W hether for culinary purposes or as a source for natural medicine, man has been using herbs for millennia. Many of them are easy to grow and some of them combine well with either vegetable plants or ornamentals.

Figure 55. Mixed herbs plug plants

Many gardeners like to have one bed in which they include all of their herbs. Whilst this might be convenient, it is not always advantageous for either the gardener or the plants. What I would suggest is that you don't shackle yourself to one method here. By all means, have a bed that is filled with herbs, but also plant them at different places in the garden or in pots. Pots can be incorporated into a patio garden or used on windowsills, where they can easily be accessed from the kitchen, but I also like to move them about the garden so that I can take advantage of their companion properties in different places.

There are thousands of herbs and at the moment we're going to focus on some of the better-known ones with which you will already be familiar. What we will be looking at from a slightly different angle to most other books is how these herbs can be used as companion plants.

Basil is a herb that every gardener and chef is familiar with. Its soft green foliage offers a wonderful peppery and slightly sweet taste when grown for its culinary advantages. That is not, however, the only reason to consider having this plant in your garden.

Basil has quite a pronounced odour, which acts as a deterrent for many flying pests, including mosquitoes and some of the insects that might be inclined to chew on neighbouring plants. You might like to try growing some alongside chilis, parsley and oregano or beans. It most classically combines, however, with tomatoes. This is a combination that offers two-way benefits. Tomatoes provide lightly dappled shade for the basil, while the basil is said to improve the taste of the fruit of the tomato. I like to plant basil among lettuce plants. They have similar watering requirements and will grow to roughly the same size, so they complement each other very well.

Figure 56. A cluster of tomatoes hangs ripening
next to purple Basil

This plant is easy to cultivate from seed, but is very sensitive to cold so you will need to bear that in mind when planting out. If you sow your seeds about six weeks before the last frost, your plants will be at the size that can be planted out in May when you are assured that the worst of the cold has passed. They prefer a free-draining soil and around six hours a day of sunshine, which is why the dappled shade of tomatoes works so well for them. Another easy propagation method is to stand a cutting in a glass of water until it roots and can then be planted directly into the garden. One of the most common varieties, and one that works very well, is Genovese. Rather than cutting the plant back to ground level when you want to harvest it, just gently snip off small handfuls of leaves as and when needed and the plant will quickly produce more.

Dill is a slightly less common herb, but one that will be familiar to people who frequently cook fish. It partners very well with tomatoes, as well as chives, thyme, lovage and lemon balm. It should not be grown with cabbage, chilis or eggplants.

Figure 57. The wonderful clusters of Dill flowers

One big no-no is to grow this plant in close proximity to carrots. They can easily cross-pollinate and result in the total loss of your carrot crop. The yellow flowers of dill are irresistible to several species of beneficial wasp, as well as to the beautiful black swallowtail butterfly. Other beneficial insects you can expect to attract include hoverflies, ladybirds and praying mantises. It is unattractive to aphids and tomato horned beetle.

This plant grows easily from seed and, once established, will self-seed itself so that you have a new supply each year. Cuttings left standing in a glass of water take very easily and allow you to determine where your plants will grow, rather than simply having to accept the freefall method of self-seeding. They have fine, feathery leaves and you can start snipping these off and using them in the kitchen as soon as the plant has half a dozen leaves established. The plant will become bushier as you cut it back.

Marjoram is a herb that seems to partner well with nearly all plants in the vegetable garden, but especially with radishes, peas, eggplants and courgettes. This really sociable herb also thrives alongside other herbs, such as basil, chives, parsley, rosemary, sage and thyme.

It comes in two basic types, one being sweet marjoram and the other the slightly smaller variety known generally as French marjoram, which is a crucial ingredient in that well-known herb mix, 'Herbs de Provence.' Its slightly sweet taste offers a variety of culinary uses. It can be added to stews, served with fish or sprinkled onto pizzas. Both varieties of marjoram are woody herbs. Sweet marjoram grows to knee height while the French variety remains slightly smaller. It appreciates full sun and a well-drained soil.

Figure 58. A great partner for most plants is the Marjoram

It is easily cultivated from seed, which can be planted directly into your beds at about one inch deep. Once the plant has established, it requires very little water and can be cut back regularly with a pair of scissors to obtain a harvest. A bunch of leafy branches can be tied together and hung upside down in an airing cupboard or other dry, well-aired space to provide dried herbs over the winter months. The flowers should be cut off as flowering seriously weakens the plant and makes it grow leggy. If you want to gather your own seed, then simply allow one or two of the plants to flower and set seed.

Mint is probably one of the better-known culinary herbs and comes in a breathtakingly large number of varieties and cultivars. It is an easy plant to grow, but can become invasive if allowed to roam freely, so I always grow mine in pots. This allows me to move them around to different places in the garden, depending on where they will grow best or where their companion benefits are most needed.

We are all familiar with the smell of mint. This powerful odour is one that even we humans have no trouble recognizing, and it is not as popular with many pests as it is with us. For this reason, it makes a wonderful companion plant that grows with just about anything in your vegetable garden.

Cabbages, cauliflower, kale and tomatoes can all benefit from being grown in the proximity of mint. Carrots, with their vulnerability to carrot fly, stand to gain particularly.

It is a versatile plant that can tolerate full sun and partial shade. It grows from underground runners and that is what makes it so invasive, so this is something that really needs to be considered. Obviously, growing your mint in pots will eliminate this threat, but if you are unable to do that, then think carefully about where you plant it. It benefits from being cut back hard, especially as it comes out of the dormant season in spring. If you are harvesting regularly, this won't be a problem, but if you aren't, then take some secateurs and cut it back from time to time.

One good feed with an organic liquid feed at the start of the growing season should be more than enough to see it through the year. If you feed this plant too much, it tends to become leggy. It will need to be watered regularly though, and you can check the soil is damp enough simply by poking your finger into it. You should feel moisture at no deeper than two inches.

Figure 59. The wonderful aroma of Fresh Mint great to use in many recipes and cocktails

In the unlikely case of needing to propagate more plants, just dig out some of the runners and cut off a length of three to four inches. Bury it in a potting mix to a depth of about an inch and soon you will have leaves popping up along the length of the runner.

Oregano is one of the more useful plants when it comes to companion planting, because it gets on with everyone and is also a culinary herb. It originates in the mountains of Greece, which tells us that it can tolerate relatively poor soils and plenty of sun. It companions particularly well with members of the brassica family, as it deters cabbage moth, and you can plant it between plants or in between rows. It also works well when grown with asparagus, peppers or tomatoes and any of the major herbs.

It is a hardy perennial, meaning that it will die back into the ground in winter and reappear early the following spring. These plants can live for up to fifteen years, but you need to know that after three to five years the potency of the leaves is noticeably diminished when used for culinary purposes. On that front, it goes well with pizza, pasta, soups and you will find it in just about any Italian recipe you care to mention.

Figure 60. Oregano partners well with almost
everything in your garden

It prefers medium soil and it doesn't really like to be fed. Water only when the soil is dry and cut it back hard when harvesting. You can do this simply by taking a pair of scissors and cutting the plant down by as much as two thirds. The leaves can either be dried or eaten fresh and they will be most powerful just before the plant flowers, though the flowers can be eaten as well.

Propagate this plant from cuttings planted into moist potting soil and allow four to six weeks for them to root sufficiently to be potted on. Alternatively, you can cut a stem, remove the bottom leaves and stand in a glass of water on a sunny windowsill until it grows its own roots.

Rosemary is another of those woody Mediterranean herbs that is versatile in the ornamental garden, in the herb garden and as a companion plant. It can tolerate very dry conditions and in addition to its fragrant leaves with their culinary benefits, it also rewards the gardener with attractive flowers that bees are passionate about. These range from pale pink right through to deep purple, depending on the cultivar or variety that you opt for.

It is a plant that combines well with any member of the cabbage family, as well as beans and peppers. When grown in proximity to tomatoes, it is said to enhance the flavour and is recognized as a plant that will increase the health of sage if it has grown nearby. It is not recommended as a companion plant for carrots, potatoes or pumpkins.

Rosemary plants can become quite big and they can live for many years, so it is important that you get the positioning right before planting. They do well in pots and just like mint, this enables the gardener to position them in different places according to requirements. This plant can be clipped quite easily to form a small but reliable hedge, and if grown around the perimeter of your vegetable garden, it creates a formidable barrier for pests to navigate, whilst at the same time, attracting pollinators.

Figure 61. Bees loving Rosemary flowers

While these plants can be grown from seed, it is a slow and unreliable process and I would recommend that you grow them from cuttings. Simply cut off a branch of new growth during the growing season and then cut below a node. Remove the lower leaves, giving yourself around two inches of bare stem and leaving a small bunch of leaves at the top so that you have a cutting that is about three to four inches long. Next, dip into rooting powder and plant the cutting into a container that contains a growing medium of two parts compost to one part vermiculite. You can plant two or three cuttings in a three-inch pot. Once your cuttings have been planted and watered, then cover the pot with a plastic bag to provide yourself with a sort of miniature greenhouse. This will ensure that humidity is maintained.

In around six weeks, the plants should have grown enough of a root system to be potted on into individual pots of their own. Tap them out of the pot, carefully separate each plant and then replant them into their own pots using the same ingredients of potting mixture as they were originally planted into. You will need to grow these plants on until they are mature enough to go into the garden and fend for themselves, but this is an easy way to rapidly multiply your plant stock. If you're doing something like growing hedges then this is certainly the most economical way to do it.

Chives are surprisingly attractive little plants that look quite similar to miniature onions and which produce very attractive, mauve flowers. I find the flower buds just prior to opening to be more attractive than the flowers themselves. Like many of the allium family, their leaves are quite pungent and this provides a strong disincentive to visits from carrot fly and aphids. For this reason, these plants partner particularly well with tomatoes and carrots. They like dappled shade, which tomato plants provide perfectly.

Figure 62. Chives flower buds

It is the leaves that provide the culinary reward and these can be harvested by simply snipping off at ground level with a pair of scissors. They are then eaten fresh or frozen until required. The bulbs will continue to grow and produce fresh leaves quite happily. Every five years or so, you will need to lift and divide them, because they become too tightly bound together. Lift them with a garden trowel in spring, separate the bulbs and then plant them again; they will soon be producing new leaves.

You can grow them quite easily by sowing them directly into a rich, well-prepared soil in spring. Once the leaves are strong enough, thin the plants to between nine and twelve inches. Alternatively, sow some seeds in three to four inch pots indoors in March and keep them relatively warm. When they start to become crowded, repot them in bunches of five to six plants per pot and once you are sure that the roots are established, you can start hardening them off outdoors during the daylight hours and bringing them in just at night. They will be ready to plant out as soon as the first frosts have passed.

Cilantro is more commonly referred to as coriander in Europe. It is a delicious herb that can be used for cooking or chopped and sprinkled fresh into salads, soups or even stews. It has a powerful flavour that is very pronounced, as is its fragrance. It plays a major role in both Indian and Asian cuisine. The flat leaves are very reminiscent of flat-leafed parsley, but one sniff of this plant will soon tell you that it is very different. Both its odour and its taste far more pronounced.

It is a deterrent against spider mite and potato beetle and therefore partners well with spinach, lettuce and other leafy vegetables, as well as potatoes. This plant is itself vulnerable to attack from aphids, so consider growing it with chervil, coreopsis or sweet alyssum, as these plants all attract aphid-eating insects such as hoverflies and ladybirds

Many gardeners will tell you that cilantro is a finicky plant to grow and I must say, I have to agree with them, although the rewards it offers are so great that I am prepared to accept some inconvenience. The problem with this herb is that if the weather gets too warm or the roots become too dry, it bolts very quickly. Bolting occurs when the plant puts out flowers and then seeds. A plant will do this very rapidly if conditions are less than ideal and it suspects it is going to die. It immediately tries to produce offspring so that the genetic line will not be lost. Clearly, cilantro is more nervous than most other herbs. When cilantro bolts, the leaf shape changes and that wonderful flavour is lost.

Figure 63. Close up of Coriander leaves

The secret to growing cilantro successfully lies in succession planting and always planting into a deeply dug and rich soil. Plants need to be kept moist and never allowed to dry out. You can sow seed directly into the ground from spring, right through until the beginning of September and ideally, you want to sow every three to four weeks, so that you have a continuous succession of healthy plants available for harvest. When the leaves are nice and bushy, cut them back to within about one to two inches of the ground and, with luck, the plant will produce more leaves.

It is the fresh leaves of this plant that make it such a culinary delight and although suppliers of culinary herbs are happy to sell you dried leaves, there is just no comparison in flavour when compared with fresh. Whilst it is possible to sow these plants indoors and then plant out the seedlings, it should be noted that they produce a taproot, so this is going to reduce your success rate. Furthermore, they grow so quickly from seed when given the right conditions that there is no great advantage to be gained from starting them off early indoors or in the greenhouse.

You can gather your own seed, which will be produced in abundance if you allow just one or two plants to flower. Another culinary advantage is that the seeds, when green, offer a lemon flavour that differs greatly from the leaves you will have been enjoying. Heat is the biggest problem with these plants and ideally, you want to be growing them at between 50 to 77°F (10 and 20°C). Don't overfeed them, but ensure that the soil into which you first sow is rich in humus, which will help retain moisture more readily.

Tarragon is a perennial herb with two very distinct varieties. The first and most commonly grown is French tarragon and the other is Russian tarragon. Russian tarragon has much coarser leaves and lacks the flavour that makes French tarragon so popular.

The problem here is that French tarragon cannot be grown from seed and therefore you will need to purchase a plant or grow from cuttings. Another method is to persuade one of your neighbours to supply you with a plant when they divide their own stock. As these plants need to be divided every three to four years, this is generally quite a good way to go about acquiring some.

Figure 64. Fresh Tarragon in an herb garden

While tarragon is a great culinary herb when used fresh, it can also be dried or frozen, but as always, this tends to reduce the flavour. Although the scent of the leaves acts as a deterrent to some insects, the main reason for growing this plant, other than as a culinary herb, is that it is believed to enhance the flavour of plants that are growing around it. The greatest example of this is eggplant/aubergine, which is said to be considerably tastier when grown in the vicinity of tarragon.

If you allow the plant to flower, this will weaken it and the best way to keep your plant in prime condition is to cut it back by two thirds when it is looking bushy and leave the remaining third to start producing new and pristine growth.

Sage is a herb that thrives in full sun. Although it will tolerate a certain amount of shade, it will never thrive in the same way that it would in a position offering full sun. A low-growing plant with fragrant leaves that deter pests, its diminutive height means that it grows well with brassicas of all kinds, as well as carrots, with which it is often interplanted, to ward against carrot fly. Many strawberry growers insist that growing sage in the vicinity of their strawberries enhances the flavour.

As a culinary herb, this one is an essential ingredient of many Mediterranean dishes, whilst in the United States and Britain, it is more commonly mixed with stuffing and served with roasted fowl of one kind or another.

It is a very easy plant to grow and, because it is a perennial, it requires little looking after once it has become established. It is often grown alongside other perennial herbs such as oregano, marjoram or parsley. In spring, the seeds can be sown outdoors at a depth of about one-eighth of an inch and with a gap of twenty-four inches between plants. It prefers a rich soil and other than that it is most fragile during the early growing stages, after which it requires little in the way of watering. A quick test of the soil in the vicinity with your forefinger will tell you if there is sufficient moisture or not.

Whilst it is still relatively unestablished, just trim off one or two leaves per plant as required for the kitchen. However, once the plant matures, it can be cut back hard and the leaves retain much of their flavour when dried. After cutting back it will bounce back quite quickly. The only major threat to this plant is from fungal diseases brought about by lack of air circulation. Don't allow plants to become too crowded and cut out any leaves that become brown or distorted. If watering does become necessary, then water at the base of the plant, rather than wetting the leaves themselves.

There are literally dozens of different varieties of this herb, ranging from deep purples right through to mixtures of yellow with white and pale green variegations. Although the more exotic-looking plants can add a splash of beauty to the garden, it is the more modest regular green leaf that will have the most flavour.

Figure 65. Sage and Thyme are a fragrant addition to your herb garden

Thyme is a delightful low-growing herb. It is an ever-green perennial and is extremely tough, so is an ideal plant to grow if you live in an area that experiences drought-like conditions. There are many different varieties, but it is important to note that there are two major divisions—ornamental and culinary. It is important to know which one of these you would prefer. Crushing some leaves between your fingers will soon tell you the difference, as the culinary variety is much more fragrant.

If you are using this plant as a companion plant, then I would suggest opting for one of the many culinary options. Its delightful little flowers attract pollinators as well as helping to deter low-flying pests and so it is useful for growing beneath plants such as broccoli, Brussels sprouts and cabbage. It also enhances the flavour of strawberries, tomatoes and eggplants/aubergines. In the kitchen, it can be used fresh or dried to augment the flavour of stews and roasts. Ornamentally, it is often grown in pots or as a ground cover and quite frequently planted between paving stones so that its aroma is shared when trodden upon.

Although it is possible, I don't suggest propagating this plant from seed. Instead, you will have much better results if you take three-inch cuttings in the spring or summer. Remove the bottom leaves and plant into a small pot of free-draining potting mix. Another quick method of reproducing plants is through layering. This involves taking a branch that is still growing on an existing plant and pinning it to the ground with a U-shaped metal staple or a simple piece of bent wire. In a matter of weeks, roots will develop where the branch is in contact with the earth and you can simply snip it off the parent plant and replant in a more suitable position.

Figure 66. Companion planting glorious shades

7

CHEMICAL INTERACTIONS

We are not always sure about the chemical interactions that take place between plants, but it would seem that some plants simply do better when they have their favourite companions growing among their community. One example of this is a combination of tomatoes and carrots. When grown together, many gardeners believe that the tomatoes produce larger fruit. This is said to also result in smaller carrots, but many gardeners prefer small carrots, because they provide a sweeter vegetable. Obviously, it would be up to you to decide whether such a result would suit your individual requirements. Another example of chemical interaction is that between beets and garlic. When grown together, it is frequently reported that the beets have a better flavour.

There are some chemical interactions that are some-what easier to understand. We know that herbivorous insects are drawn to the plants that they feed on through several different mechanisms. One of these is a chemical scent that the target plant puts out. By combining the target plant with other plants that have their own odours, it is sometimes possible to disrupt the attack of most common pests. If the companion plant also provides shelter for insects that predate upon the herbivorous pest, then a secondary benefit is achieved.

Figure 67. An urban vegetable garden with a wide variety of produce

Plant contradictions

As in most societies, we find that some plants are just better at socialising than others. Broccoli is one of those plants that both vegetables and fruit seem happy to grow alongside. Quite why that is, nobody is sure, but one of the suggestions is that broccoli repels some of the pests that favour fruit and vegetables.

Not all plants in the community that you are attempting to create, however, are going to be quite so amenable to one another. Asparagus, for example, is a heavy feeder, and when grown in the vicinity of potatoes or onions, deprives them of nutrients that they need to reach their maximum potential. For exactly the opposite reason, it is never recommended that you grow beans alongside tomatoes or peppers. Tomatoes and peppers are both happy to grow in low nitrogen conditions. As the beans bind nitrogen into the soil, this can result in diminished fruit on the tomatoes and peppers.

Coriander and dill are both so similar that they cross-pollinate easily and the resulting plants never fare well and do not produce the desired herbal advantages that created the cross. Fennel is a popular plant with gardeners, but is regarded as cantankerous and unsociable by other members of the vegetable community. It seems to inhibit the growth of tomatoes and beans as well as many other vegetables and when designing your garden, it is recommended that you let this herb have a place of its own, where it will grow quite happily as a grumpy old hermit.

Surprisingly, potatoes can be very antisocial plants. When grown in the vicinity of tomatoes, they slow the tomato production down and at the same time, themselves become more vulnerable to a disease known as Phytophthora. In fact, when rotating crops, it is not a good idea to plant tomatoes where potatoes have been the previous season, or vice versa. Other plants that don't get on well with potatoes include turnips, sunflowers, as well as vine crops such as melons, cucumbers and squash.

The reasons that some plants don't grow well in community is that they may be allelopathic. This means that they emit chemicals from their roots that are deliberately intended to discourage other plants from growing in their vicinity. This is part of an evolutionary process in which plants attempt to eliminate competition from nearby plants. A powerful example of this is the black walnut tree, and it is really not worth attempting to grow vegetables beneath this tree.

Lettuces are relatively tolerant plants, but they don't seem to grow happily when closely combined with parsley. Although the usually benign and easy-going cucumber is a favourite with many gardeners, being so easy to grow, if you plant cucumbers alongside tomatoes, potatoes, cauliflower or some of the stronger smelling aromatic herbs, they can easily become coy and fail to set fruit.

Figure 68. A modern well planned vegetable garden with raised beds and assorted vegetables

In many instances, it is quite easy to understand why some plants don't get along. Dill and carrots, for example do not thrive together, because of their very similar nutrient requirements. Why garlic and onions seem to resent the growth of beans remains somewhat more of a mystery. As I mentioned earlier, much of what we know about companion planting is anecdotal and the amount of scientific research in this regard is somewhat limited. That does not mean that the perceived relationships between these plants is not valid. It merely means that we don't understand all of the reasons that some plants seem to thrive in community, whilst others prefer to remain more aloof.

As you are probably beginning to realise, the list of companion plants, as well as those that are less inclined to grow well together, can be quite extensive. The charts in the appendix will offer more suggestions. As a gardener, this is a large subject to get to grips with and to start off with, it will probably be easiest to base your planting plans on those charts. After that, I suggest that you keep careful records so that you can assess both your successes and your failures to the point where you are gradually able to build up a record that is applicable to your own garden.

There are certain rules of thumb that, although general, will help you when selecting plants to create a community. Try to pair a plant with others that have similar requirements in terms of moisture and sunlight. At the same time, however, don't pair your plant with another that is going to compete for the same nutrition. When using plants to deter pests, it is always better to grow them as close to the threatened plant as possible. For example, if you don't keep your marigolds close to the plants that you are trying to protect, the insect pests will probably just go right around them to reach your precious vegetables.

Above all, try to break the old gardener's habit of growing your plants in monoculture formations. All this will do is provide a more easily identifiable target for insect pests. It is true that when we grow plants in rows, as we have become accustomed to doing, then cultivation procedures such as watering and feeding become easier. That is why this method is so popular with large-scale commercial farmers. However, your objective differs very much from that of the large-scale commercial grower. You want a diverse range of crops, whilst at the same time, you are attempting to create an environment that is both friendly to your plants and the ecosystem. It is a different way of thinking and one that we are only just starting to get used to after years of being exposed to neat vegetable patches where each crop had its place. There, regulated growing formations thrive because they fall under the protection of chemical pesticides. As a gardener whose priority is to remain organic, you do not have that luxury and so you are obliged to use different methods. Remind yourself constantly that good horticultural practices outweigh the benefits that chemicals can provide. In the next chapter, we will take a more in-depth look at pest control without the use of toxic chemicals.

8

KNOW WHO YOUR FRIENDS ARE

I imagine many of my readers will have noticed by now that there is one theme that recurs quite frequently when referring to the subject of companion planting—the desire to attract beneficial insects. Beneficial insects can be crucial to organic gardening, because they provide a powerful element of pest control, as you are unable to simply use toxic chemical controls.

In order to garden successfully without pesticides, you need to become something of an amateur entomologist, because otherwise, it is almost impossible to differentiate friend from foe. In this chapter, we will be taking a look at some of the main players who will assist you in your fight against pests. It is certainly not a totally comprehensive list, as to compile one in an arena where there are so many insect species would be a mammoth undertaking. I do recommend that you get hold of a book or use the internet so that you can identify who your comrades are. Once you are able to recognise them, it will make your life much easier and there really aren't that many. It is a fascinating subject and one which will augment your gardening skills considerably.

Ladybirds. Ladybirds are probably one of the most iconic creatures in the insect world. From an early age, most children are be able to point out a ladybird with its bright red body and very pronounced spots. What many people don't realise is that there are over 6000 different types of ladybird worldwide and that the familiar red bodied beetle with its black or white spots is just one of many colours that these little guys come in. They can range in colour from yellow, right through to black. Contrary to common belief, the number of spots indicates different species and is not related to the age of the insect.

In the US, ladybirds are often referred to as ladybugs, although this is, in fact, a misnomer, because ladybirds are beetles and not bugs. Beetles tend to be omnivorous, whereas bugs feed exclusively on plant material and have mouths designed for piercing and then sucking the juice out of plants.

Ladybirds feed on a wide range of garden pests, ranging from aphids through to scale insects, but also including some caterpillars and even spider mites.

Figure 69. Ladybug on Apple blossom

People are familiar with the brightly coloured ladybird in its adult form, but far fewer people are able to recognise the very differently shaped larva of this beetle, which is an even more vociferous consumer of pests such as aphids.

They look like miniature alligators and very often the female beetle will lay her eggs either amongst a colony of aphids or in a vicinity that she suspects they will soon

Figure 70. Ladybug larvae

inhabit. By doing this, she is able to ensure that her offspring will have a supply of food readily available when they hatch.

The beetles themselves hibernate over the winter months, emerging when the weather warms, to continue foraging through the plants of fortunate gardeners and aiding in the war against pests.

They feature strongly in children's stories, nursery rhymes and mythology and throughout the world, and many cultures are superstitious about killing them. A ladybird can eat up to five thousand aphids over its lifetime and the larva can eat up to forty aphids every hour, so it is easy to see why it is advantageous to make them welcome wherever you garden.

Lacewings These delicate-looking little creatures generally have green bodies and clear, see-through wings with veins running through that that look like lace and from which their common name is derived. Their larvae are fierce predators of aphids, caterpillars, mealybugs and even scale insects.

Figure 71. The see-through clear wings give the name to these wonderful insects

Worldwide there are more than 2000 different species. Most of them lay in the region of 600 eggs over the period in which they are adults. It is the tiny emerging larva that offers the most benefit to the gardener. Adults are just over a half-inch long and they survive in their adult form for three to four weeks. The larva has two pairs of hollow jaws and with one they capture their unsuspecting prey, whilst with the other, they suck out its bodily juices. Each tiny larva will consume in the region of 200 aphids per day. I'll let you do the calculation as to how many aphids could be removed if you were to have just a few laying adult lacewings in your garden.

Spiders I have met many people who cannot stand spiders and who are sometimes quite afraid of them. For the green-minded gardener, however, the spider is a wonderful creature to have living in your garden. Worldwide, there more than 45,000 different species of spider and even in your garden you probably have more than half a dozen different species present, though you may not realise it.

Spiders have different tactics when it comes to capturing their prey. Some are active hunters; others build intricate web systems and some position themselves in flowers and then pounce on their prey when it lands nearby. There are very few spiders that will bite a human being and they will only do so if you accidentally disturb them. Of the more than 40,000 species, there is only a handful that are sufficiently venomous to cause death in humans. Trying to differentiate one spider from another may be a bit of a difficult undertaking and instead, I welcome all spiders into my garden. They eat a huge variety of pests, ranging from caterpillars right through to aphids, wasps and flea beetles. Many of them even eat mosquitoes. To my knowledge, there are none that actively harm plants, so as far as I am concerned their presence works entirely in my favour.

Praying mantises are another easily identifiable garden predator. They will eat many different types of garden pest, including aphids, whiteflies and crickets. They are hunters who catch the prey in their barbed forelegs before eating it, normally headfirst.

Figure 72. Praying Mantis standing tall on a leaf

They have the rare ability to turn their heads 180° and have excellent vision, in part due to the fact that they have five eyes. A little-known fact is that they only have one ear but that it is able to detect ultrasonic sound which enables them to take evasive action and avoid bats. That ear is on their belly, of all places. Apparently, this causes sound to resonate more.

Some people will debate whether or not having these insects in your garden is beneficial or not. They are voracious hunters and they are not picky eaters, meaning that they will eat beneficial insects as well as insect pests. It is up to each gardener to decide for himself what line to take on this particular argument, but my own feeling is that their presence is an indication of a healthy ecosystem and I am more than happy to let them stay.

Hoverflies are small flies with yellow and black bands that give them an appearance quite similar to a wasp. They feed on nectar and pollen and so can help to pollinate your garden plants, but once again it is the larvae that offer the most benefit to the gardener.

The adults lay their eggs individually in places where they see colonies of aphids. The tiny larva then hatches and although almost invisible to the naked eye, immediately sets about consuming the aphids in its vicinity.

Soldier beetles are common in many gardens. They have elongated bodies and red to brown wings with a black dot in many species. They are sometimes referred to as leather beetles or leather wings and the name soldier beetle relates to the fact that some of the red-coloured species matched the uniforms once worn by British soldiers.

Once again, it is the larvae of these beetles that offer the most benefit in the garden. They are ferocious predators of many soft-bodied insects, but most noticeably aphids. People who don't know their

Figure 73. Leather Beetles are beneficial soldiers for your garden

insects may look at this beetle and assume that it is a pest, because the adults are often seen on flowers. In fact, it is because the adults feed on pollen that they are on the flowers and so they provide a certain amount of pollinating as they go about their day-to-day lives.

Establishing balance:

There are companies that specialise in selling beneficial insects to both the domestic gardener and agricultural businesses. You place an order for a specific species and then it will simply be mailed to you through the post. Depending on your chosen insect and the time of year, you may be sent eggs, ready hatched larvae or adults, and then you simply need to release them into your chosen site in the garden.

This may be a tempting road down which to travel, especially if you are of an impatient nature. I have never found it necessary to do this. In fact, I have always been amazed at how quickly insect life moves in when the habitat is free of toxic chemicals.

If you are anxious to augment the number of insect allies you have living in your garden, you would be better off ensuring ideal conditions rather than forking out money where it may not be necessary. Here, things can become a little counterintuitive. By nature, we have become a species that thrives on tidiness. That doesn't necessarily correlate well with what insects may regard as perfect living conditions. They thrive in places where there are piles of leaves and garden debris. If you have been gardening for a little while, you will have learned that if you leave a few logs or piles of leaves for any length of time in your garden, it will soon be inhabited by a wide variety of different insects.

The important thing to take away from all of this is that your garden needs to become an ecosystem in its own right. Every time you deprive that ecosystem of a specific species and replace it with another, you are tampering with a natural process. Buying in a thousand lacewings may seem to offer an almost instant solution to your aphid problems, but you are distorting natural process that you may be better off allowing to evolve in their own particular way. I appreciate that merely by gardening we are producing more than a natural amount of certain varieties of plants, be they edible or ornamental. That in itself is part and parcel of the gardening game. At the same time, I like to allow the underlying natural processes to take place with as little interference on my part as possible. This is never an instant process and unfortunately, we have grown up in a world in which instant results have become almost obligatory.

Nature simply cannot be rushed. Your own private ecosystem will take a few years to settle down and find its own balance. During that time, you may well suffer a certain amount of frustration as one pest or disease seems to gain the dominant hand. Over time, however, the good forces such as predatory insects will build up and the natural balance will be achieved, if you allow it to be.

9

THE ORNAMENTAL GARDEN

In this book, we have focused our attention mainly towards the vegetable and herb growing regions of the garden. This is, indeed, where most companion planting takes place, but I definitely believe that the same principles can be applied just as effectively in the more ornamental parts of the garden. I will touch on it briefly here to offer you some suggestions you may find useful. This region is, after all, often subjected to many of the same pests and diseases as the rest of the garden.

When laying out the ornamental garden, the gardener is faced with a huge variety of choices and problems, including the colour spectrum, shape and form and the necessity for one plant to start flowering just as another starts to go over. We will look at all these possibilities much later in the series when we deal with garden design. For the moment, when I refer to companion planting in the ornamental garden, I want to look at it in exactly the same way as we have looked at it in the previous chapters. In other words, as we take a brief look at companion planting beds and borders, we are going to be following similar principles to those that we have followed so far. We are looking to create synergy in the garden and to develop an ecosystem that is balanced enough for us to abandon the use of toxic chemicals.

Figure 74. English style cottage garden view in summer with blooming peonies and companions

There are many people who consider the use of pesticides in the ornamental garden as legitimate, because they not going to be eating the produce coming from that area. That thinking is actually quite shortsighted. For example, if you spray the aphids on your roses, there is every possibility that they'll be consumed by ladybird larvae, which will then die. Those larvae formed the beachhead for the next generation of ladybirds and so you have reduced the size of your army. It may well be that your vegetable garden and ornamental garden are totally separate entities, but that is only in your opinion. Nature will not recognise those boundaries between one area and another and those ladybirds that are breeding in the ornamental garden are highly likely to eventually migrate to the vegetable garden. The whole area needs to be seen as a single entity and any harm done to the fauna in one part of it will in turn affect the fauna in another. If you truly wish to follow organic principals, you need to cease the use of chemicals throughout your garden. We gardeners have enough problems with the insect population being reduced if our neighbours do not adhere to our principles or if nearby agricultural businesses don't see pesticides as a cause for concern.

Many of the plants that we have discussed in the previous sections of this book will produce exactly the same benefits in the ornamental garden as they would in the vegetable or herb garden. Where things become a little more complicated is that we are now looking for a visual effect and some of those plants could well clash with what we are trying to achieve either from a colour or form perspective.

Figure 75. A stunning visual effect created with lavender and rose shrubs

An example of this would be roses. These very popular garden plants are prone to infestations of aphids and for that reason, they do very well when grown alongside plants such as onions and garlic. I have no problem in introducing vegetables to the ornamental garden, because I believe that many vegetables are just as attractive as some of those plants we more traditionally associate with flowerbeds and borders. For many, however, this is a step too far, so we need to look at an alternative to plant with our roses. Often, the taller roses produce their flowers and much of the foliage quite high up the plant, leaving the lower areas quite exposed and often not looking particularly appealing.

Plants like lavender, catmint, and rosemary are able to fill that gap between soil level and the higher sections of the rose, while at the same time offering a deterrent to common pests or encouraging the presence of predatory insects. Many of the different roses look very good with these plants growing beneath them. We now have a situation where we have plants complementing each other, not only visually, but also in terms of pest control. If none of those three plants combines well with your planting scheme, then why not consider sweet alyssum, chives or some of the many ornamental alliums? Shrub roses can benefit and look good when underplanted with a carpet of thyme.

Figure 76. Beautiful blooming herbal garden

Almost all of the herbs that we have so far discussed will thrive in the ornamental garden and bring with them all of the companion planting benefits that they currently offer in the vegetable garden. Many of them are wonderfully attractive and will enhance the ornamental garden, while at the same time providing that little extra flavour in the kitchen. The wise gardener might consider abandoning the herb garden and instead incorporating all of their herbs into the ornamental garden.

In a series of tests, it was found that mixed hedging around agricultural fields encouraged colonisation by large numbers of predatory insects. These insects were happy to travel large distances across the fields in search of their prey. That obvious benefit can easily translate to our home gardens. In many ornamental gardens, we see wide use of hedges, but very infrequently are they made up of a variety of different species. Instead, we have grown accustomed to monoculture hedging, often using non-native plants such as leylandii. Not only are these non-native plants of little interest to local insects, but in recent years, a disease affecting that particular plant has meant that some gardeners have lost their hedges altogether. Had they been using mixed hedging, that situation could have been avoided, whilst at the same time creating an ideal habitat for predatory insects and birds, which we know play such an important role in our gardens.

Many of the best-known ornamental plants or exotics have been imported from different parts of the world. They bring with them many very attractive properties, but they are often not adapted to cope with either pests or disease in the foreign conditions in which they suddenly find themselves living.

Figure 77. Charming mix of traditional and exotic plant for this garden edged with conifers and green shrubs

Often there are indigenous plants that are equally attractive, but which have become overlooked, simply because we now fail to recognise their beauty. Familiarity has blinded us to how attractive they can be. Perhaps it is time to start re-evaluating some of the indigenous plants that are available to us. When woven into a well-thought-out planting scheme, these natives often perform just as well as more exotic plants. In doing so, they bring with them a hardiness that can only be found in plants that have evolved under local conditions.

Indigenous plants are familiar to local fauna and therefore are instantly more attractive as habitat. In addition, indigenous plants are already adapted to local conditions and therefore are far less prone to disease, drought or pests that could easily damage exotic plants. In the Western Cape of South Africa, one of the seven plant kingdoms of the world, gardening was strongly influenced by exotic plants introduced by the early English colonisers. It is only in recent years, as they have been hit repeatedly by severe droughts, that many of the local plants are now being recognised as better candidates for the garden. I'm not suggesting that you do away with your beloved roses or imported daffodils altogether. What I do recommend is that you find an indigenous nursery near you and consider incorporating these plants into your existing scheme. It will have a dramatic effect on the ecosystem and synergy that you are trying to develop.

Earlier in the book, we looked at the subject of allelopathic plants. These are plants that produce toxins to
discourage other plants from competing with them,
and the black walnut is one of the most common examples. In the ornamental garden, there are several plants
that do the same thing and whilst this doesn't mean that
you shouldn't use them, you need to be aware of their
capabilities and the fact that you may not be able to
grow the plants in the immediate vicinity. Examples of
this are the English laurel, sumac, rhododendron,
forsythia, goldenrod and sambucas. This sort of natural
plant protection is not something that you should be
overly concerned about. Very often, the plant will
exude these chemicals, either from the roots or leaves,
to protect itself from competition from its own seeds,
such as in the case with the sunflower. When looking to
partner plants in the ornamental garden, it is a good
idea to run the plant name along with the word "allelopathic" through your computer, just to see if this is
likely to become an issue.

CONCLUSION

Companion planting can be a slightly confusing subject and there can be no denying that part of the reason for that is that it is not an exact science. Whilst gardeners have been practicing companion planting for hundreds of years, there has only been a limited amount of scientific research done on this vast subject and much of the information we have is based on tradition, folklore and hearsay. At the same time, we should not disregard these practices simply because concrete evidence for them is scant. We need to bear in mind that there are a limited number of plant scientists and that much of the funding for research comes from agriculture, rather than the domestic gardening arena.

I would really encourage you to try some of the combinations that you have just read about, but also to try out plant combinations of your own. There are so many variables here that it is very difficult to take them all into account. The specific climate you are dealing with, the type of soil you have and the varieties of pests that you need to contend with, will all fall into one big boiling pot that will make your own situation and experience unique.

Figure 78. Fresh Tomato and Lettuce in nontoxic vegetable garden

One of the biggest hurdles that has to be overcome when converting from gardening with chemicals to organic gardening is that of instant results. If your roses are attacked by aphids or your cabbages are infested with caterpillars, the results will quickly be seen if you use any sort of chemical toxin against these pests. In the organic environment, change is far less obvious and that frustrates many gardeners and deters them from going down this road. I can empathise with those gardeners who are becoming exasperated at seeing their crops or their flowerbeds infested with pests. Here, I have to urge you to look at the bigger picture. What you're doing when you garden organically is creating a balanced environment. It will never be one in which you totally annihilate pests or disease, but that balance does improve over time. It is unrealistic to expect this momentous change to occur overnight.

What I have learnt, and what I'm desperate to share with you, is that over time, the natural ecosystem that builds up reaches a point where I am able to grow and harvest very nearly as much as I could before I became fully organic. In addition, I can now rest assured that the food I put on my table has not been contaminated with toxic chemicals and that I am no longer harming the environment that I am responsible for. Whether we like it not, we are now slowly being forced to a point where we have to recognise that we humans are not independent of the natural environment that surrounds us. The sooner we accept that, the sooner we can start to reverse some of the incredible harm we have done to the natural world.

Those readers who have been following this series of books will know that I do not portray organic gardening as being easier than gardening with chemicals. I also admit that in some cases there may be lower yields. I have been doing this for a long time now, and I really have no regrets about having changed the philosophy behind my gardening techniques. Companion planting is just one of many tools I use to enhance my skills, not only as a gardener but also as a custodian of a small ecosystem that I call my garden. It is my sincere hope that you too will be encouraged to go down the same route. Over time, you will reap the rewards, not only in terms of the plants, vegetables and fruit that you produce. You will start to spot an increase in the number of predatory insects that take up residence alongside you, your soil will become healthier and rich in earthworms and the bird population will explode.

Please don't feel that you are either a companion planter or not. It is not an either-or situation. In some places in the garden, companion planting may work for you, while in others, it may not. This may be due to any number of different factors. You may have limited space, the aesthetics might not appeal to you, or you simply might not have the time to plant anything other than a small variety of plants. The beauty of this method is that it is scalable. You can put in a few pest deterrents here or some flowering plants to attract pollinators there and gradually build up. As you see things start to work, you will hopefully feel more encouraged to expand the use of this technique.

Gardening is one of the few areas in our modern lives where we are able to give something back to nature instead of taking from it. It is difficult to place a value on that, especially in a world where so much as measured by the yardstick of dollars and cents. Every now and then, we find an opportunity to add value that doesn't conform to the world's recognised economic criteria. I believe that organic gardening is one of those opportunities.

Figure 79. Freshly harvested organic vegetables

Thank you so much for reading my book

"Beginners Guide To Companion Planting".

If you have enjoyed reading this, and perhaps picked up a new trick or two, please could you leave a star rating or a review for me on Amazon? Reviews really help me create more books that help gardeners produce a tastier, bigger and more efficient yield all year round.

Use this link: https://relinks.me/1913871150

or scan this QR code below:

Thank you so much.
Peter Shepperd

ABOUT THE AUTHOR

 Peter Shepperd is in his 40s and his interest in gardening started when he decided to give his family access to fresh, homegrown and organic food. Peter has been studying new gardening approaches to diversify his experience and skillset.

His experimentation has allowed him to figure out what works and what definitely doesn't. He disagrees with the use of pesticides and chemicals.

He has decided to produce this series of books to cover all aspects of growing, gardening and organic sustainability.

Peter has spent over a decade experimenting with different gardening techniques and perfecting his approach to growing fruits, vegetables, herbs and other plants. Not only this, but he has learnt how to make the most of each part of the food that he grows.

Teaching others has become his passion as some affordable, and straightforward practices have entirely transformed how his family gets access to healthy, delicious, nutritious and attainable food. Peter's vision is to slowly transition more and more people away from the often-tasteless vegetables that are purchased in supermarkets and are heavily reliant on the use of chemicals that are damaging the environment, towards home-grown organic healthy produce, believing that the process of doing so will also help grow the person that has produced them as well.

Peter lives with his family near Windsor in England.

THE BOOKS CURRENTLY IN THE GREEN FINGERED GARDENERS SERIES™

REFERENCES

Figure 1. Mazurowska K.(Young onion, lettuce, onions, rucola, beans and beets, in vegetable permaculture cultivation. Eco-friendly backyard garden, vegetable garden. [photograph]. *Shutterstock.*

https://www.shutterstock.com/image-photo/young-onion-lettuce-onions-rucola-beans-752049907

Figure 2. Cheepphoto. Rice field and a azolla fern or water fern at organic rice farm. [Photograph]. *Shutterstock.*

https://www.shutterstock.com/image-photo/rice-azolla-fern-water-organic-farm-1266817576

Figure 3. Hanson H. 920130. Corn plant bean flower planting. [Photograph]. *Pixabay.*

https://pixabay.com/photos/corn-plant-bean-flower-farming-381956/

Figure 4. Maylee. (2020). Pink and yellow flower in tilt shift lens. [Photograph]. *Unsplash.*

https://unsplash.com/photos/Z1Z2ryY3Zkc

Figure 5. Congerdesign. (2017). White cabbage garden vegetables. [Photograph]. *Pixabay.*

https://pixabay.com/photos/white-cabbage-garden-2521700/

Figure 6. S. Hermann & F. Richter. (2018). Field Nature. [Photograph]. *Pixabay.*

https://pixabay.com/photos/sunflower-field-nature-summer-3540277/

Figure 7. Göschel P. (2018). Borage cucumber herb. [Photograph]. *Pixabay.*

https://pixabay.com/photos/borage-cucumber-herb-borretschblüte-3595293/

Figure 8. Goellner A. (2019). Corn vegetable garden. [Photograph]. *Pixabay.*

https://pixabay.com/photos/corn-vegetable-garden-grow-4262081/

Figure 9. Calvet B.E. (2019). Kitchen garden. [Photograph]. *Unsplash.*

https://unsplash.com/photos/fCw8v41elGk

Figure 10. Spike M. (2018). Urban gardening locavore. [Photograph]. *Unsplash.*

https://unsplash.com/photos/w5DqWoZ5_YM

Figure 11. Turner P. Companion Planting of Home Grown Organic Potatoes (Solanum tuberosum) and Poached Egg Plants or Meadowfoam (Limnanthes douglasii) on an Allotment in a Vegetable Garden in Rural Devon, England, UK. [Phootograph]. *Shutterstock.*

https://www.shutterstock.com/image-photo/companion-planting-home-grown-organic-potatoes-1455511769

Figure 12. Pasja1000. (2018). Relaxation spring reading. [Photograph]. *Pixabay.*

https://pixabay.com/photos/relaxation-spring-reading-heart-3359535/

Figure 13. Lees D. (2020). Poached egg flower bloom. [Photograph]. *Pixabay*.

https://pixabay.com/photos/poached-egg-flower-bloom-garden-5087062/

Figure 14. Pershina M. (2017). Cosmetic oil natural. [Photograph]. *Pixabay*.

https://pixabay.com/photos/cosmetic-oil-natural-cosmetic-3164684/

Figure 15. MrGajowy3. (2019). Marigold flower yellow. [Photograph]. *Pixabay*.

https://pixabay.com/photos/marigold-flowers-yellow-nature-4304736/

Figure 16. Groschen A. (2020). Soup Nasturtium flower. [Photograph]. *Pixabay*.

https://pixabay.com/photos/soup-nasturtium-flower-leaves-5480400/

Figure 17. Silviarita. (2018). Soap calendula marigold. [Photograph]. *Pixabay*.

https://pixabay.com/photos/soap-calendula-marigold-flowers-3809466/

Figure 18. McBride-Kennedy M. (2017). Butterfly purple. [Photograph]. *Pixabay.*

https://pixabay.com/photos/lavender-butterfly-purple-flowers-2829707/

Figure 19. Majikhands. (2020). Chives flower herb. [Photograph]. *Pixabay.*

https://pixabay.com/photos/garlic-chive-flowers-herbs-chives-4992967/

Figure 20. Elisa28diamonds. (2019). Crimson clover plant. [Photograph]. *Pixabay.*

https://pixabay.com/photos/crimson-clover-plant-flowers-bloom-4242717/

Figure 21. Кудрявцева Н. (2017). Artemisia picture. [Photograph]. *Pixabay.*

https://pixabay.com/photos/sagebrush-2360542/

Figure 22. Landmesser B. (2020). Sage leaves in garden. [Photograph]. *Unsplash.*

https://unsplash.com/photos/ked7OTkMNC0

Figure 23. Capri23auto. (2018). Composites asteraceae. [Photograph]. *Pixabay.*

https://pixabay.com/photos/zinnia-composites-asteraceae-3579960/

Figure 24. Van Der Maaten J. (2020). Yellow flower in macro lens. [Photograph]. Pexels.

https://www.pexels.com/photo/food-flowers-summer-garden-4989593/

Figure 25. Tantetati. (2020). Flower close up. [Photograph]. *Pixabay.*

https://pixabay.com/photos/flowers-close-up-pink-nature-4868375/

Figure 26. wal_172619. (2018). Sunflower bird picture. [Pixabay]. *Pixabay.*

https://pixabay.com/photos/tit-sunflower-food-birds-4388255/

Figure 27. Kalee S. (2020). Nepeta Faassenii "Six Heels giant".[Photograph]. *Pixabay.*

https://pixabay.com/photos/nepeta-faassenii---six-hills-giant-5273916/

Figure 28. Richter M. (2020). Lathyrus Latifolius pea blossom. [Photograph]. *Pixabay.*

https://pixabay.com/photos/lathyrus-latifolius-pea-blossom-5275757/

Figure 29. Shazna F. (2021). Flower plant white. [Photograph]. *Pixabay.*

https://pixabay.com/photos/alyssum-flowers-plant-white-flowers-6141333/

Figure 30. Karathanasis I. (2019). Green asparagus. [Photograph]. *Pixabay.*

https://pixabay.com/photos/green-asparagus-asparagus-green-4501429/

Figure 31. Verburg H. Outdoor permaculture garden with companion planting of Corn and Green beans plants. [Photograph]. *Shutterstock.*

https://www.shutterstock.com/image-photo/outdoor-permaculture-garden-companion-planting-corn-1869829519

Figure 32. Tkaczuk J. The beetroot - purple beet, also table beet, garden beet, red and golden chard. Growing in the veg garden. [Photograph]. *Shutterstock.*

https://www.shutterstock.com/image-photo/beetroot-purple-beet-table-garden-red-1922188991

Figure 33. Muller H. M. (2021). Green plant in macro lens photo. [Photograph]. *Unsplash.* https://unsplash.com/photos/9qt0QKk_N3M

Figure 34. Eelffica. (2014). Cabbage garden floral. [Photograph]. *Pixabay.* https://pixabay.com/photos/cabbage-garden-floral-plants-440018/

Figure 35. Watson S. Healthy young beetroot, onions and carrot plants growing in a home vegetable garden, Christchurch, New Zealand. [Photograph]. *Shutterstock.* https://www.shutterstock.com/image-photo/healthy-young-beetroot-onions-carrot-plants-1621172800

Figure 36. De La Colina Flores S. M. (2019). Orchard vegetables. [Photograph]. *Pixabay.* https://pixabay.com/photos/cucumber-orchard-vegetables-food-4643417/

Figure 37. Alkemade. (2019). Leek vegetable harvest. [Photograph]. *Pixabay.*

https://pixabay.com/photos/leek-vegetable-harvest-food-4480380/

Figure 38. Price S. (2018). Lettuce salad food. [Photograph]. *Pixabay.*

https://pixabay.com/photos/lettuce-salad-food-healthy-greens-3582434/

Figure 39. Kenan Kitchen. (2018). Green leafed plant near trees. [Photograph]. *Unsplash.*

https://unsplash.com/photos/Bbq3H7eGids

Figure 40. Matchou. In the associated crop garden - row of parsnips surrounded by carrots, in front of a row of white borage - top view. [Photograph]. *Shutterstock.*

https://www.shutterstock.com/image-photo/associated-crop-garden-row-parsnips-surrounded-1962661054

Figure 41. Turcic P. Marigolds protecting potatoes. [Photograph]. *Shutterstock.*

https://www.shutterstock.com/image-photo/marigolds-protecting-potato-516673225

Figure 42. Verburg H. Outdoor permaculture garden with companion planting of Corn, Green beans and Pumpkin plants. [Photograph]. *Shutterstock.*

https://www.shutterstock.com/image-photo/outdoor-permaculture-garden-companion-planting-corn-1869829522

Figure 43. Shannon M. Genova basil and sungold tomatoes Companion planting helps confuse insects seeking tomatoes to eat . [Photograph]. *Shutterstock.*

https://www.shutterstock.com/image-photo/genova-basil-sungold-tomatoes-companion-planting-1881210406

Figure 44. Katie1824. (2018). Root earth agriculture. [Photograph]. *Pixabay.*

https://pixabay.com/photos/root-earth-agriculture-nature-leaf-3360870/

Figure 45. Hobson M. Courgettes and Beans growing on an allotment in summer. [Photograph]. *Shutterstock.*

https://www.shutterstock.com/image-photo/courgettes-beans-growing-on-allotment-summer-1896425014

Figure 46. Zakic D. (2019). Close up photography of bumblebee. [Photograph]. *Unsplash.*

https://unsplash.com/photos/s58GuIVFaaM

Figure 47. Hlaváč M. (2020). Red apple fruit on tree branch. [Photograph]. *Unsplash.*

https://unsplash.com/photos/W9ikwhGIXGM

Figure 48. LoggaWiggler. (2013). Quince fruit plant. [Photograph]. *Pixabay.*

https://pixabay.com/photos/quince-fruit-plant-leaf-tree-65192/

Figure 48. Pexels. (2016). Japanese cherry blossom. [Photograph]. *Pixabay.*

https://pixabay.com/photos/japanese-cherry-blossom-flowers-tree-1839982/

Figure 49. Fox A. (2021). Plant leaves foliage. [Photograph]. *Pixabay.*

https://pixabay.com/photos/plant-leaves-foliage-6281457/

Figure 50. Free-Photos. (2015). Lemon trees. [Photograph]. *Pixabay.*

https://pixabay.com/photos/lemon-tree-lemons-tree-citrus-801996/

Figure 51. Moore J. (2018). Nature flower flora. [Photograph]. *Pixabay.*

https://pixabay.com/photos/nature-flower-flora-leaf-summer-3320518/

Figure 52. Yazdi J. (2019). Green fruits. [Photograph]. *Unsplash.*

https://unsplash.com/photos/OZ94M5lYVMY

Figure 53. Ilona F. (2019). Peach fruit ripe bio. [Photograph]. *Pixabay.*

https://pixabay.com/photos/peach-fruit-ripe-bio-sweet-4396313/

Figure 54. Turner P. Companion Planting of Fruit Trees, Flowers and Home Grown Organic Vegetables on an Allotment in a Vegetable Garden in Rural Somerset, England, UK. [Photohgraph]. *Shutterstock.*

https://www.shutterstock.com/image-photo/companion-planting-fruit-trees-flowers-home-1471961816

Figure 55. Smith R. (2019). Green leaves on brown wooden table. [Photograph]. *Unsplash.*

https://unsplash.com/photos/liOlTBljpdA

Figure 56. Wolf J. An atomic grape tomato plant is pruned to a single stem supported on a trellis with plastic clips and heavy fishing line. A cluster of tomatoes hangs ripening next to purple basil. [Photograph]. *Shutterstock.*

https://www.shutterstock.com/image photo/atomic-grape-tomato-plant-pruned-single-1768424858

Figure 57. Alekseeva S. (2021). Dill umbrellas, close up. [Photograph]. *Unsplash.*

https://unsplash.com/photos/2scH7iT8nhs

Figure 58. S.B. (2020). Origanum Vulgar. [Photograph]. *Pixabay.*

https://pixabay.com/photos/marjoram-origanum-vulgar-5340400/

Figure 59. Grabowska K. (2020). Green leaves plant. [Photograph]. *Pexels.*

https://www.pexels.com/photo/green-leaves-plant-4599920/

Figure 60. Patriot R. (2018). Oregano herb plant cooking. [Photograph]. *Pixabay.*

https://pixabay.com/photos/oregano-herb-plant-cooking-flower-3506914/

Figure 61. Sawalali. (2019). Rosemary bee flower. [Photograph]. *Pixabay.*

https://pixabay.com/photos/rosemary-bee-flowers-herbs-nature-5613409/

Figure 62. Congerdesign. (2021). Herbs chives garden culinary. [Photograph]. *Pixabay.*

https://pixabay.com/photos/herbs-chives-garden-culinary-herbs-6299151/

Figure 63. Lynn B. (2020). Close up shot of cilantro. [Photograph]. *Pexels.*

https://www.pexels.com/photo/close-up-shot-of-cilantro-5884935/

Figure 64. Michal_R. Fresh tarragon in a herb garden. [Photograph]. *Shutterstock.*

https://www.shutterstock.com/image-photo/fresh-tarragon-herb-garden-305989841

Figure 65. SilviaRita. (2019). Herbs garden plant. [Photograph]. *Pixabay.*

https://pixabay.com/photos/herbs-green-plant-garden-gardeners-4108058/

Figure 66. Hope J. (2021). Herb garden. [Photograph]. *Unsplash.*

https://unsplash.com/photos/96zlc1Bt51w

Figure 67. Gardens by design. An urban vegetable garden with a wide variety of produce. [Photograph]. *Shutterstock.*

https://www.shutterstock.com/image-photo/urban-vegetable-garden-wide-variety-produce-618774416

Figure 68. Gardens by design. A modern well planned vegetable garden with raised beds and assorted vegetables. [Photograph]. Shutterstock.

https://www.shutterstock.com/image-photo/modern-well-planned-vegetable-garden-raised-1236053068

Figure 69. Christiane. (2012). Ladybug apple blossom. [Photograph]. *Pixabay.*

https://pixabay.com/photos/ladybug-apple-blossom-branch-722783/

Figure 70. Frühauf C. (2020). Larvae ladybug. [Photograph]. *Pixabay.*

https://pixabay.com/photos/larva-ladybug-5149377/

Figure 71. Artsehn. (2013). Lacewing insect fly. [Photograph]. *Pixabay.*

https://pixabay.com/photos/lacewing-insect-fly-green-1744767/

Figure 72. Houska L. (2016). Praying mantis insect leaf. [Photograph]. *Pixabay.*

https://pixabay.com/photos/praying-mantis-insect-leaf-mantis-1170776/

Figure 73. Cocoparisienne. (2014).Red weichkafer beetle. [Photograph]. Pixabay.

https://pixabay.com/photos/red-weichkäfer-beetle-396412/

Figure 74. Evseyeva M. beautiful english style cottage garden view in summer with blooming peonies and companions - stachys, catnip, heranium, iris sibirica. Composition in white and blue tones. Landscape design. [Photograph]. *Shutterstock.*

https://www.shutterstock.com/image-photo/
beautiful-english-style-cottage-garden-view-
1911931192

Figure 75. Salcedo J. Colorful garden border, white
fence and pink roses. [Photograph]. *Shutterstock.*

https://www.shutterstock.com/image-photo/colorful-
garden-border-white-fence-pink-44072212

Figure 76. Tkaczuk J. Beautiful blooming herbal garden
with chives, lavender, rosemary, mint, catnip and many
others. Herbal and Medicinal plants Garden. [Photo-
graph] . *Shutterstock.*

https://www.shutterstock.com/image-photo/
beautiful-blooming-herbal-garden-chives-lavender-
1669520509

Figure 77. Evgeniya B. Beautiful garden with palm
trees. Emerald green color. View of a well maintained
garden newly mown lawn edged with conifers and
green shrubs. Miniature charming birdhouse. [Photo-
graph]. *Shutterstock.*

https://www.shutterstock.com/image-photo/
beautiful-garden-palm-trees-emerald-green-
1738325294

Figure 78. Sonthong A. Fresh Tomato and Lettuce in Nontoxic Vegetable Garden. [Photograph]. *Shutterstock.*

https://www.shutterstock.com/image-photo/fresh-tomato-lettuce-nontoxic-vegetable-garden-605432222

Figure 79. Morinka. Closeup of freshly harvested vegetables (turnips, beetroots, carrots, round marrow), top view. [Photograph]. *Shutterstock.*

https://www.shutterstock.com/image-photo/closeup-freshly-harvested-vegetables-turnips-beetroots-307161773